Thus Shalt Thou Serve

An Exposition of the Offerings and
the Feasts of Israel

by

Charles W. Slemming

Thus Shalt Thou Serve

An Exposition of the Offerings and
the Feasts of Israel

by

Charles W. Slemming

CHRISTIAN ❖ LITERATURE ❖ CRUSADE
Fort Washington, Pennsylvania 19034

CHRISTIAN LITERATURE CRUSADE

U.S.A.
P.O. Box 1449, Fort Washington, PA 19034

with publishing programs also in:
GREAT BRITAIN
51 The Dean, Alresford, Hants. SO24 9BJ

AUSTRALIA
P.O. Box 419M, Manunda, QLD 4879

NEW ZEALAND
10 MacArthur Street, Feilding

ISBN 0-87508-566-0

Copyright © Mrs. Hilda Slemming

First American edition 1974
This revised edition 1999

*Dedicated to my wife
in acknowledgment of her great help
in preparing the manuscript.*

Scripture quotations are from the
Holy Bible, New King James Version.
Copyright © 1982 by Thomas Nelson, Inc.

Printed in the United States of America

Preface

MUCH has been said concerning the tabernacle in the wilderness. It is a subject that has held a fascination for many Bible students, and yet in itself it is not complete.

One does not go to church these days to admire the architecture of the building, beautiful as some of them may be; nor yet to enjoy the comfort of the pews, for most pews are uncomfortable enough. Neither does one go to church merely for the fellowship of friends, although this is rewarding. We go to church in order to worship God, to sing His praises and to benefit from His Word.

Thus it was with the tabernacle. Interesting as it might have been as a structure, it was the service of the tabernacle that mattered. Having written books on the tabernacle and on the priestly garments, we now add a third book to the series which, we trust, will bring enlightenment on the offerings and the feasts—some of the ritual of the early Jewish worshipers. From these subjects we desire to see what God requires of us in our worship in these New Testament days.

This book has been divided into two parts. Part I is concerned with the five Levitical offerings and Part II deals with the Sabbath and the seven feasts of the Lord. The subjects may be studied separately if desired. We trust that they may prove instructive and a blessing to the reader. We send this book on its way remembering that "all Scripture is given by inspiration of God, and is profitable."

Yours in the love of His Word,
C. W. SLEMMING
London, 1965

Contents

Part I
A Living Sacrifice
or *The Five Levitical Offerings*

Part II
Your Reasonable Service
or *The Feasts of the Lord*

Part I

A Living Sacrifice

or

The Five Levitical Offerings

· Chapter 1 ·

Introduction

A GREAT PORTION of the book of Leviticus is devoted to the subject now coming under consideration. While the offerings all belonged to the immediate lives of the people and were observances, they were also commemorative, and had future fulfillment in the history of Israel. Beyond that, they foreshadowed some of the greatest doctrines of the Church.

The offerings, with one exception, were sacrificial and required the shedding of blood. This was because they were figurative of the one sacrifice that was to be made once in the end of the age in the death of the Lord Jesus Christ. The feasts, however, were not sacrificial but ceremonial. They revealed the present and future conduct of the Hebrew people because they were, or would be, the people of God. We might define the two, therefore, by stating that the offerings were Godward and the feasts manward; or, as we have stated in another book, the offerings reveal man's walk *to* God through sacrifice, and the feasts declare man's walk *with* God through separation from wickedness.

In all of these offerings, with their minute detail, we discover that nothing was left to man's imagination or interpretation; rather, everything hung on his obedience. The illustrations are perfect, requiring no additions or subtractions.

The holiness of God demanded a sacrifice.

The majesty of God required certain regulations.

The honor of God necessitated a code of conduct.

The perfection of God expected the best of its kind.

The purity of God deserved freedom from blemish.

The sovereignty of God called for absolute obedience to detail.

Multiple offerings were necessary because no one offering could give a complete picture of the perfect offering made at the end of the age, or cause us to understand all the significance, meaning, and blessings that were to come to the children of men from the one great and complete offering by our Lord Jesus Christ upon the cross of Calvary. Each was inadequate in itself, so five offerings revealed five different aspects of the one offering:

> Leviticus 1 describes the Burnt Offering.
> Leviticus 2 describes the Grain Offering.
> Leviticus 3 describes the Peace Offering.
> Leviticus 4 describes the Sin Offering.
> Leviticus 5 describes the Trespass Offering.

In addition to the details given in the first five chapters of Leviticus, chapters 6 and 7 add the law of the offerings. Nothing was left to man's fancy or to human imagination. Every detail was dictated by God to Moses.

While the offerings are given in the order stated, we note that this was not the order in which they were observed. That was:

(1) Burnt Offering.
(2) Grain Offering.
(3) Sin Offering.
(4) Trespass Offering.
(5) Peace Offering.

This change of order holds no significance with many people. Some may not have noticed that there was a difference. Others consider it to be making "much ado about nothing," suggesting that Moses on different occasions wrote the offerings down as they came into his mind, as one might jot down a shopping list from week to week. To this attitude it must be pointed out that "*all* Scripture is given by inspiration of God," not according to man's memory or the failure of that memory. So when things have an exact repetition in the Bible, we should take note of the fact; and when variations reveal themselves, these are just as noteworthy. This is particularly important in these early chapters of Leviticus because there appears to be so much repetition . . . about which Matthew 6:7 says: "But when you pray, do use not vain repetitions as the heathen do: for they think that they will be heard for their many words." As the Bible does not contradict itself, whenever repetition is found one may be sure that it is not "vain." Therefore the reason must be found.

In this change of order, the peace offering, which was third in the list, became fifth in the observance. It must be the last of the five because peace comes as a result of obeying all the others. Peace is effect, not cause. The reason that it is third in the catalog is because the five offerings are divided into two categories. The first three are called sweet aroma offerings, which means that they were voluntary. As the peace offering was voluntary, it is moved up with the other two in that class. Noah's offering was also one producing a soothing aroma (Gen. 8:21). The last two offerings were compulsory. God demanded a sin offering and a trespass offering.

As surely as there was an order in which the offerings were observed, so there was an order for the feasts, for God is a God of order. This is well established in nature as well as in His Word. Paul commanded the church to do all things "decently and in order" (1 Cor. 14:40).

Leviticus has always been considered a dry and uninteresting book, and not without reason. But so are many of the everyday things of life and of nature —until we see them under the microscope. Have you ever seen common salt, sugar, or any other ordinary crystals, under a microscope? If not, you still have a great experience awaiting you. Have you seen grass, and the many minute forms of plant life which grow around us, under the microscope? If you have, you will know that these are some of those things of beauty which are a joy forever! It is our intention to put these truths of God's Word under the microscope of His Holy Spirit and to behold a detail and a wonder that some have never dreamed would be in the Bible, much less in the Old Testament.

To simplify the studies, we will consider:

(1) *The Nature of the Offering*—that is, the animals used and why they were chosen.

(2) *The Offerer's Work.*

(3) *The Priest's Work.*

Then we will note:

(4) *God's Portion.*

(5) *The Priest's Portion.*

(6) *The Offerer's Portion.*

And finally we will look at:

(7) *The Typical Teaching*, as each offering points to that one Offering, the Lord Jesus Christ.

(8) *The Symbolism*, as it applies to the life of the believer.

All Scripture having been given by inspiration of God, the little details are as important as the great principles. Scanning the Bible may show its beauty and bring some satisfaction, but scrutinizing the Bible shows its wonder and creates a tremendous fascination. This is why we are encouraged to "search the Scriptures," to "compare scripture with scripture," to "be diligent to present ourselves approved to God."

· Chapter 2 ·

The Burnt Offering

Now the Lord called to Moses, and spoke to him from the tabernacle of meeting, saying, "Speak to the children of Israel, and say to them, 'When any one of you brings an offering to the Lord, you shall bring your offering of the livestock—of the herd, and of the flock.

'If his offering is a burnt sacrifice of the herd, let him offer a male without blemish; he shall offer it of his own free will at the door of the tabernacle of meeting before the Lord. Then he shall put his hand on the head of the burnt offering, and it will be accepted on his behalf to make atonement for him. He shall kill the bull before the Lord; and the priests, Aaron's sons, shall bring the blood, and sprinkle the blood all around on the altar that is by the door of the tabernacle of meeting. And he shall skin the burnt offering and cut it into its pieces. The sons of Aaron the priest shall put fire on the altar, and lay the wood in order on the fire. Then the priests, Aaron's sons, shall lay the parts, the head, and the fat in order on the wood that is on the fire upon the altar; but he shall wash its entrails and its legs with water. And the priest shall burn all on the altar as a burnt sacrifice, an offering made by fire, a sweet aroma to the Lord.

'And if his offering is of the flocks—of the sheep, or of the goats—as a burnt sacrifice, he shall bring a male without blemish. He shall kill it on the north side of the altar before the Lord; and the priests, Aaron's sons, shall sprinkle its blood all around on the altar. And he shall cut it into its pieces, with its head and its fat; and the priest shall lay them in order on the wood that is on the fire upon the altar; but he shall wash the entrails and the legs with water. And the priest shall bring it all, and burn it on the altar; It is a burnt sacrifice, an offering made by fire, a sweet aroma to the Lord.

'And if the burnt sacrifice of his offering to the Lord is of birds, then he shall bring his offering of turtledoves, or young pigeons. The priest shall bring it to the altar, wring off its head, and burn it on the altar; its blood shall be drained out at the side of the altar. and he shall remove its crop with its feathers and cast it beside the altar on the east side, into the place for ashes. Then he shall split it at its wings, but shall not divide it completely; and the priest shall burn it on the altar, on the wood that is on the fire. It is a burnt sacrifice, an offering made by fire, a sweet aroma to the Lord.'" (Lev. 1:1–17)

Then the Lord spoke to Moses, saying, "Command Aaron and his sons, saying, 'This is the law of the burnt offering: The burnt offering shall be on the hearth upon the altar all night until morning, and the fire of the altar shall be kept burning on it. And the priest shall put on his linen garment, and his linen trousers he shall put on his body, and take up the ashes of the burnt offering which the fire has consumed on the altar, and he shall put them beside the altar. Then he shall take off his garments, put on other garments, and carry the ashes outside the camp to a clean place. And the fire on the altar shall be kept burning on it; it shall not be put out. And the priest shall burn wood on it every morning, and lay the burnt offering in order on it; and he shall burn on it the fat of the peace offerings. A perpetual fire shall burn on the altar; it shall never go out.'" (Lev. 6:8–13)

THIS FIRST OFFERING is called the burnt offering: "The burnt offering shall be on the hearth on the altar all night until morning, and the fire of the altar shall be kept burning on it. . . . And the fire on the altar shall be kept burning on it; it shall not be put out. And the priest shall burn wood on it every morning, and lay the burnt offering in order on it; and he shall burn on it the fat of the peace offerings. A perpetual fire shall burn on the altar; it shall never go out" (Lev. 6:9–13).

This offering is also called a sweet aroma offering (Lev. 1:9 and 13). The sweet aroma offering signified a freewill offering. That statement is confirmed in Leviticus 1:3, ". . . he shall offer it of his own free will."

While the offerings display the work that Christ accomplished upon the cross for the sinner as He dealt with his sin and his trespasses, and established his peace, yet we find in the burnt offering that Christ first meets God's holiness and satisfies His demands. He is "offering Himself without spot to God," doing the will of the Father, satisfying all His claims without any reservation on the Lord's part. In satisfying God's demands, secondly He meets man's need. This is why it is called a "whole burnt offering." It was given to God in its entirety, man having no share in it. At the same time it teaches that we in turn must surrender our best—yes, our all—seeking only to please Him who has called us. It is only to the extent to which we yield our all to Him that we shall learn to appreciate that we are receiving His all in our lives. To the measure with which we seek to please Him, we shall know those pleasures which are forevermore.

The Nature of the Offering—*According to possession. Bulls, sheep, goats, turtledoves, pigeons.* "If his offering is a burnt sacrifice of the *herd*, let him offer a male without blemish . . ." (Lev. 1:3). "And if his offering is of the *flocks*—of the sheep, or of the goats—as a burnt sacrifice, he shall bring a male without blemish" (Lev. 1:10). "And if the burnt sacrifice of his offering to the Lord is of *birds*, then he shall bring his offering of turtledoves or young pigeons" (Lev. 1:14).

In each instance the animal was domestic, a creature that was tame and fed on vegetation, as against the wild animal and those that fed on carrion. Only the docile creature could represent the pure and holy One who gave His life a ransom for many. The animals had to be free from blemish as they prefigured the One who was free from sin.

Many today would denounce the idea of slaying an innocent animal, even though we slay innocent humans through our careless and selfish behavior on the highways and appear to have no remorse for our appalling conduct. Man will murder his fellowman in retaliation for the smallest injustice done to himself, or perhaps because he desires excitement, and the law will do all it can to excuse the murderer. The religious views of the people of the world and their behavior are exceedingly conflicting, and even while some say that the shedding of blood should be removed, they are finding fault with Cain because he did not do that very thing. But the story of Cain and Abel reminds us that the slaying of an innocent animal existed long before the laws of Leviticus. As sin had already robbed man of life, nothing short of life could be the remedy.

Which of these animals should be offered by any particular offerer was not a matter of choice. The offering was . . .

According to possession. If the social standing of the offerer were such that he was the possessor of a *herd*, then he offered a bull. God would not accept a lamb from him. If, however, the offerer did not possess a herd but he did have a *flock,* then his offering must be a sheep or a goat. Should the offerer be of the poor of the land, having neither a herd nor a flock, then the offering should be of *birds*—turtledoves or young pigeons. This latter was the offering made by Mary, the mother of Jesus, at the time of her purification, which is one of the indications that Jesus was born of poor parents.

The lesson is that God expects man to give to Him in the measure that He has prospered him. He does not accept inferior gifts from those who have possessions, and neither does He expect from His people gifts, service, or anything that they do not possess. Our responsibilities are measured according to our privileges, not more than we have, not less than we have, always the best of what we have— without blemish.

In one instance there was an alternative, turtledoves or young pigeons. There might be little or no difference as to the monetary value of these birds. The alternative was available because at certain times of the year one or other of these birds would be out of season. It would then be tough and inedible. When they were of no use to man, they were of no use to the Lord. The birds had to be given when they were in season. Unless a thing costs us something it is worth nothing.

This is a very important lesson to learn. Man today is seeking to give God the things he no longer wants. The worn suit or the out-of-fashion dress are sent to the missionary. The unwanted furniture and the threadbare carpet are sent to the church for a rummage sale. Or a man waits until he has made his fortune and has all that his heart desires and then he will offer his remaining years to the Lord's service. We are not suggesting that God cannot, or will not, use those years, but to the young man we would say: "Give your life while it is in season, with its energies and powers, and while the mind is clear and alert." And to the older people we would say, since the missionary has given her all, could we not give her a new dress or something that is worthwhile? God asks for firstfruits, not leavings—for that which costs, not for that which is paltry; for that which honors His name, not that which is an insult. "'You offer defiled food on My altar. But you say, "In what way have we defiled You?" By saying, "The table of the Lord is contemptible." And when you offer the blind as a sacrifice, is it not evil? and when you offer the lame and sick, is it not evil? Offer it then to your governor! Would he be pleased with you? Would he accept you favorably?' says the Lord of hosts" (Mal. 1:7–8). "'And you bring the stolen, the lame, and the sick; thus you bring an offering! Should I accept this from your hand?' says the Lord" (Mal. 1:13). "And the King will answer and say to them, 'Assuredly, I say to you, inasmuch as you did it to one of the least of these My brethren, you did it to Me'" (Matt. 25:40).

The Offerer's Work—*Identification*. ". . . he shall offer it of his own free will at the door of the tabernacle of meeting before the Lord" (Lev. 1:3).

This statement not only means that it was offered as a freewill gift, with no compulsion or pressure being put on the offerer (and compulsion always robs one of the joy of giving or the joy of service), but there is a marginal reading (see the NASB): "that he may be accepted before the Lord." Comment has just been made on the quality of the gift. It is that which registers the quality of the giver. While the gift is important, the giver is more important to God—"that *he* may be accepted."

"Then he shall put his hand on the head of the burnt offering, and it will be accepted on his behalf to make atonement for him" (Lev. 1:4). The significance of this action is that he laid his hands firmly upon the living animal, as one would press firmly upon the seal of a document to leave the thumb imprint. It is identification. The animal was about to die, but before it did, the offerer identified himself with the living creature because he was going to be identified with the dead animal. In other words, he was recognizing that *he* was the one who should die and that this animal was his substitute.

Then he slew the animal. The offerer, or the sinner, is always the person responsible for death, for had there been no sin there would have been no death. "Therefore, just as through one man sin entered the world, and death through sin, and thus death spread to all men, because all sinned . . ." (Rom. 5:12).

With the bulls and the birds there is no indication as to the exact spot of the sacrifice, but with the sheep it is stated that death was imposed on the north side of the altar. There is no reason why we should not believe that they were all slain in the same place. It is not necessary to make a repetition of words. However, the lamb is more specifically the type of Christ who was the Lamb of God, the One who took away the sins of the world, and He died on the north side of the city of Jerusalem. Calvary is located to the north of Jerusalem. It is amazing to see this detail in the law that was given 1,300 years before Christ died; and more amazing that the religious leaders of Christ's day, who were so steeped in the law, did not recognize the fulfilling of these scriptures. When the god of this world blinds men's eyes, they are surely blinded! Only the Lord can remove those scales.

The Priest's Work—*Sprinkling blood.* ". . . and the priests, Aaron's sons, shall bring the blood and sprinkle the blood all around on the altar that is by the door of the tabernacle of meeting. And he shall skin the burnt offering, and cut it into its pieces. The sons of Aaron the priest shall put fire on the altar, and lay the wood in order on the fire. Then the priests, Aaron's sons, shall lay the parts, the head, and the fat in order on the wood that is on the fire upon the altar; but he shall wash its entrails and its legs with water. and the priest shall burn all on the altar as a burnt sacrifice . . ." (Lev. 1:5–9).

Because Christ is the Burnt Offering, yielding His all to the satisfaction of the Father, Aaron's sons would here point to the Church of Jesus Christ. As priests unto God and as sons of the great High Priest, that Church is the priestly household.

The priest had quite a duty to perform in this offering. He had to . . .

(1) Sprinkle the blood all around on the altar (Lev. 1:5).

(2) Skin the burnt offering (Lev. 1:6).

(3) Cut it into its pieces (Lev. 1:6).

(4) Put fire on the altar, and lay the wood in order on the fire (Lev. 1:7).

(5) Wash the entrails and the legs (Lev. 1:9).

(6) Burn all on the altar (Lev. 1:9).

(7) Wring off the head of the bird (Lev. 1:15).

(8) Remove its crop and feathers (Lev. 1:16).

(9) Put on his linen garments (Lev. 6:10).

(10) Carry the ashes outside the camp (Lev. 6:11).

The believers, having accepted that the blood of Jesus Christ (and the life is in the blood) has satisfied a holy God on their behalf, do not store that blood as some private possession, but they, as priests, must distribute it around in a way that others may see and recognize the same truth and the same blood that has brought them cleansing. However, we do not, and must not, scatter it just anywhere as something thrown away, because the blood is holy. It is precious; it must be kept within the sanctity of divine things.

Men were not permitted to eat blood because of the life that is in it. Maybe the thought in mind can be clarified if we consider the name of Jesus. This is precious on the lips of believers, but when that name is scattered around in the outside world it often becomes a name used in blasphemy.

The skinning of the animal exposed the whole of the viscera and revealed that, within as well as without, it was free from blemish. Then the priest had to cut it into its pieces. This was not a chopping or a hacking of the carcass in some crude fashion, but a careful dissecting of the animal—the head, the entrails, the legs—to make sure that each part was free from any blemish. These parts were representative:

The head—the seat of the mind and the intellect.

The entrails—the will and the affections.

The legs—the outward walk and conduct.

The fat—health and virility.

When Christ, our offering, was thus examined, the results were:

In Him was no sin (1 John 3:5).

He knew no sin (2 Cor. 5:21).

He committed no sin (1 Pet. 2:22).

He was without sin (Heb. 4:15).

God said concerning His Son: "This is my beloved Son, in whom I am well pleased." He satisfied His Father in thought, in word, in deed, in walk. We, too, as the Church, are encouraged to examine the nature and person of Christ as revealed in the

Word. If we examine the head, we shall see that He came not to do His own will but the will of the Father. If we consider the fat, it tells of His devotion and His affection—finding them devoid of selfish interest. If we consider the inner organs—the heart, the lungs, the kidneys, the liver—each doing a perfect job to maintain a perfect body, they would represent in Christ a heart of compassionate love and lungs of purity. And the legs or limbs speak of a perfect walk.

Having been established as free from blemish, the sacrifice was then placed carefully and in order upon the fire and burned. Since there was no reservation, no imperfection, no selfish motive, and no self-glorification in Christ, God allowed Him to die, thereby satisfying His holiness.

The sacrifice of the burnt offering having been completed, the priest then had to dress in special garments and carry the ashes outside the camp to a clean place. Ashes are the result, or the fruit, of burning. These were carried with care to a special place because they had a special purpose. Salvation is the fruit of Christ's work on the cross. It must be acknowledged, propounded, kept separate from all else, by the Church because it and it alone can bring cleansing for the sinner.

God's Portion—*All that was burned.* That was the whole dissected carcass because it was a whole burnt offering; there was no reservation. It was the full consecration of the Lord Jesus Christ to God, the complete yieldedness of the Son to the Father. The other offerings were shared in one way or another;

and yet, while this must remain true, there was . . .

The Priest's Portion—*The hide*. Doctrinally, all belonged to God. In type, the priest had a portion inasmuch as he had a participation in the ceremony. The Word of God teaches: "Do you not know that those who minister the holy things eat of the things of the temple, and those who serve at the altar partake of the offerings of the altar? Even so the Lord has commanded that those who preach the gospel should live from the gospel" (1 Cor. 9:13–14); also, ". . . the laborer is worthy of his wages" (Luke 10:7).

The priest, therefore, received the hide (Lev. 7:8), which is not referred to after the animal was skinned. It did not become part of the offering that was put on the fire and, therefore, not part of the "all that was burned." The hide was the evidence that the animal had existed. It was also the evidence of a sacrifice because there cannot be a hide without a sacrifice. Would not this skin, the only property of man, take our minds back to the Garden of Eden and to the skin which God provided for a covering for Adam and Eve?

The Offerer's Portion—*Nothing*. The offerer shared only in one offering, the peace offering. As a sinner, man has no participation in the work of redemption because salvation is not the result of our works but of His work.

The Typical Teaching—*Christ our Passover. Surrender of self:* As no one offering could give a full-length portrait of the great offering, the Lord Jesus Christ, five offerings were needful to reveal five aspects of His perfect work. The burnt offering, as the first of these five offerings, reveals the work of the Son toward the Father before the work of the Savior toward mankind. It is the complete consecration of the whole being of the Son of God to the will, mind, and purposes of God, which brought complete satisfaction to the heart of God. Said Jesus: "For I have come down from heaven, not to do My own will, but the will of Him who sent Me" (John 6:38). "My food is to do the will of Him who sent Me, and to finish His work" (John 4:34). ". . . Christ also has loved us, and given Himself for us, an offering and a sacrifice to God for a sweet-smelling aroma" (Eph. 5:2). ". . . how much more shall the blood of Christ, who through the eternal Spirit offered Himself without spot to God, purge your conscience from dead works to serve the living God?" (Heb. 9:14).

The Symbolism—*Consecration of self.* This is the truth as it applies itself to mankind, or what God intends us to understand from the pictures He draws and the demonstrations He performs.

In the burnt offering it was the complete and entire consecration of the offerer to God. As Jesus offered Himself to God without any reservation, so in turn must we do the same thing. Thus the apostle declared: "I beseech you therefore, brethren, by the mercies of God, that you present your bodies a living sacrifice, holy, acceptable to God, which is your reasonable service" (Rom. 12:1). "For you were bought at a price; therefore glorify God in your body and in your spirit, which are God's" (1 Cor. 6:20).

Man takes one step at a time not only in his comprehension of spiritual things but also in his

Christian walk. We must acknowledge that steps must be taken in the right order. The first step is always before the second step. To stand on the top rung of the ladder, a person must mount the lower rungs one by one. To stand in the place of spiritual reception and enjoy all that God is giving, we must first surrender our whole being in a complete yieldedness to the Lord, as Jesus yielded Himself without reserve to His Father.

· Chapter 3 ·

The Grain Offering

"When anyone offers a grain offering to the Lord, his offering shall be of fine flour. And he shall pour oil on it, and put frankincense on it. He shall bring it to Aaron's sons, the priests, one of whom shall take from it his handful of the fine flour and oil with all the frankincense. And the priest shall burn it as a memorial on the altar, an offering made by fire, a sweet aroma to the Lord. The rest of the grain offering shall be Aaron's and his sons'. It is a most holy offering of the offerings to the Lord made by fire.

"And if you bring as an offering a grain offering baked in the oven, it shall be unleavened cakes of fine flour mixed with oil, or unleavened wafers anointed with oil. But if your offering is a grain offering baked in a pan, it shall be of fine flour unleavened, mixed with oil. You shall break it in pieces, and pour oil on it; it is a grain offering. And if your offering is a grain offering baked in a covered pan, it shall be made of fine flour with oil. You shall bring the grain offering that is made of these things to the Lord. And when it is presented to the priest, he shall bring it to the altar. Then the priest shall take from the grain offering a memorial portion, and burn it on the altar. It is an offering made by fire, a sweet aroma to the Lord. And what is left of the grain offering shall be Aaron's and his sons'. It is a most holy offering of the offerings of the Lord made by fire.

"No grain offering which you bring to the Lord shall be made with leaven, for you shall burn no leaven nor any honey in any offering to the Lord made by fire. As for the offering of the firstfruits, you shall offer them to the Lord, but they shall not be burned on the altar for a sweet aroma. And every offering of your grain offering you shall season with salt; you shall not allow the salt of the covenant of your God to be lacking from your grain offering. With all your offerings you shall offer salt.

"If you offer a grain offering of your firstfruits to the Lord, you shall offer for the grain offering of your firstfruits green heads of grain roasted on the fire, grain beaten from full heads. And you shall put oil on it, and lay frankincense on it. It is a grain offering. Then the priest shall burn the memorial portion: part of its beaten grain and part of its oil, with all the frankincense, as an offering made by fire to the Lord." (Lev. 2:1–16)

"This is the law of the grain offering: The sons of Aaron shall offer it on the altar before the Lord. He shall take from it his handful of the fine flour of the grain offering, with its oil, and all the frankincense which is on the grain offering, and shall burn it on the altar for a sweet aroma, as a memorial to the Lord. And the remainder of it Aaron and his sons shall eat; with unleavened bread it shall be eaten in a holy place; in the court of the tabernacle of meeting they shall eat it. It shall not be baked with leaven. I have given it to them as their portion of my offerings made by fire; it is most holy, like the sin offering and the trespass offering. All the males among the children of Aaron may eat it. It shall be a statute forever in your generations concerning the offerings made by fire to the Lord. everyone who touches them must be holy." (Lev. 6:14–18)

ALTHOUGH this is called the "meat offering" in the Authorized Version—in America commonly called the King James Version—it was the only offering of the five that made no use of flesh whatsoever. Instead the ingredients were cereal. The reason for using the word "meat" was that, in the days when King James ruled England (the days when this version was prepared), a person would not be asked out to a "meal." He would be invited to "meat." Some of the earlier updatings of the Authorized Version speak of this as a "meal offering" (the ASV, 1901) or a "cereal offering" (RSV, 1952).

Three different expressions are used in describing the offerings. They are "sacrifice," "oblation," and "offering." All of these have their place, and are not merely alternatives meaning the same thing.

Sacrifice. This always involved the shedding of blood. Living animals full of life and free from blemish were slain. This signified a life surrendered.

Oblation. This had nothing to do with blood, and referred to the offering of grain, flour, cakes, and the first fruits of harvest. (All recent non-Catholic translations, however, have dropped this Latin-based word and instead read "offering.")

Offering is a general term expressive of both, inasmuch as both were offered by one person to another.

The usual Hebrew word for offering or oblation is *minchah*, meaning "the gift of an inferior to a superior." The word is sometimes translated "present," as in the "present" sent by Jacob to Esau, also the "present" to Joseph from his brothers. *Minchah* is likewise translated "offering" in the story of Cain and Abel.

Two of these references must be enlarged upon in order to establish the full meaning of this word *minchah* because it affects biblical interpretation. Let us repeat that *minchah* means "the gift of an inferior to a superior," for it will be appreciated that such a gift must be worthy of the one to whom it is presented. If the gift were to be made to the Queen of England, or to the President of the United States of America, it must be worthy of the person or of the office held. Better give no gift than one that is inferior, because then it becomes an insult.

Jacob was commanded by God to return to his homeland and his family. On his way he learned that Esau was coming to meet him and that he was accompanied by 400 men. This was the Esau whom Jacob had twice wronged and from whom he had earlier fled. He was now fearful of the brother from whom he had stolen both blessing and birthright. Jacob prayed to God and confessed his unworthiness but asked for the Lord's delivering grace. After that he prepared a present for his brother (Gen. 32:13). This present was the same *minchah* of our study. The instructions given by Jacob to his servants, when they met Esau and offered his gift, were: "They are your *servant* Jacob's. It is a *present* sent to my *Lord* Esau" (Gen. 32:18). This was the first time that Jacob had humiliated himself before Esau. It is true that fear was the motive, but we are establishing the meaning of *minchah*, the offering we are preparing to study.

There is yet another valuable lesson to learn. It is in the story of Cain and Abel. It is generally held that God accepted the offering of Abel because of the blood and rejected the offering of Cain because the fruit of the earth was an evidence of works. However, the facts of the case do not really support this interpretation.

(1) There is no biblical evidence that Adam and Eve ever offered a sacrifice.

(2) There is no biblical evidence that God had required one up to that moment.

(3) Cain and Abel were the children of Adam and Eve, so we are still at the very beginning of the human race.

(4) The coats of skin were God's provision, not His requirement at that juncture.

(5) The word *minchah* is used with regard to the offerings of both Cain and Abel.

(6) If we assert that "the fruit of the ground" was what represented works, then surely sheep are the results of the labors of a shepherd as fruit is the result of the toil of the farmer!

What the Lord wants us to learn from this account is not the quality of the offering but the character of the offerer. ". . . Cain brought an offering of the fruit of the ground . . ." (Gen. 4:3). "Abel also brought of the firstlings of his flock and of their fat" (Gen. 4:4). The fat was the choicest part of the animal and was always required by God, as is repeated in Leviticus. Everything in the two verses suggests that Cain took the first fruit to come to hand while Abel with care chose the best of his flock. If one reads carefully the rest of the verse, he will discover that this is the fact of the case: "And the Lord respected Abel and his offering." God did not accept Abel *because* of his offering. God received the offering because of *Abel*. He was a man with a right heart and a right motive, and God does not look on the outward appearance. He looks on the heart.

With this as introduction, let us now consider the grain offering.

The Nature of the Offering—*According to property. Uncooked flour, unleavened cakes, roasted grain.* In each offering there were alternatives, not for the convenience of the offerer, as might be supposed, but according to the circumstances of the offerer, and, of course, according to the command of God.

Uncooked flour, or flour in the raw. As it was received so it could be given, remembering that this offering typified service. Man can give back to God. He has life, he may give it to God; he has time, he may give a portion; he has a Bible, he can read it; he can attend church, sing with the congregation, contribute to the collection, give a little service here and there which he feels capable of doing. God will accept these.

Unleavened cakes. Here some effort had been applied to turn the flour into something that was edible and tasty and something that could be shared with others. The life here has become a yielded life, the time given is made as effective as can be. The Bible is not just read, it is studied, kneaded, mixed with experience—making it appetizing food. Church attendance becomes church service. The voice is developed so that it can be used to God's glory. It could find its way into the choir for others to share the enjoyment. It is no more dropping a coin into the plate but learning to tithe. It is not the odd job but the dedicated service. This is more acceptable to God. All this is to be done without the leaven of pride or self-esteem.

Roasted grain. That which is preserved by fire. The faith that has stood the fire of trial, the promises of God that have been tested and tried, the life that has come through severe temptations and proved God to be faithful—these are things which rejoice the heart of God. ". . . that the genuineness of your faith, being much more precious than gold that perishes, though it is tested by fire, may be found to praise, honor, and glory at the revelation of Jesus Christ" (1 Pet. 1:7).

As in the burnt offering, so in the grain offering there is a division of requirement concerning the offerer. In the first it was according to possession, in the second it was . . .

According to property. What he offered was determined by the circumstance of possessing an *oven, a pan* (baking pan), or a *frying pan.*

Attached to these offerings were certain restrictions. "No grain offering which you bring to the Lord shall be made with leaven, for you shall burn no leaven nor any honey in any offering to the Lord made by fire" (Lev. 2:11).

No leaven. Leaven—yeast—is always a type of sin. It is that which, when brought into contact with fire, throws the lump into risings and commotions. The fermenting properties of leaven reduce the whole of the cakes into a condition of corruption. "Do you not know that a little leaven leavens the whole lump? therefore purge out the old leaven, that you may be a new lump, since you truly are unleavened" (1 Cor. 5:6–7). " 'How is it you do not understand that I did not speak to you concerning bread?—But you should beware of the leaven of the Pharisees and the Sadducees.' Then they understood that He did not tell them to beware of the leaven of bread, but of the doctrine of the Pharisees and of the Sadducees" (Matt. 16:11–12).

Do not overlook that in this grain offering service is being considered more than salvation. There was no selfish intent, no malice, no evil thought in the ministry of Christ, since there was no sin in Him. Likewise, for the believer there must be no malice in his life and no ill motive in his service. Everything must be done with singleness of purpose if it is to be accepted by God.

No honey. Honey, although sweet to the taste, if taken in excess can turn sour in the stomach. The pleasures of life are only for a season; they soon fail. "It is not good to eat much honey" (Prov. 25:27). Dr. V. Raymond Edman points out that roasted barley without sweetening is flavorless. The things that speak of Christ's suffering must not have man's ideas added to them in order to make them more palatable to us. It is necessary constantly to remind oneself of what it meant to Him, the Holy One, to bear away our sin. If we, as Christians, would spend more time contemplating what it cost Him for our redemption, we would spend less time counting how much it costs us to serve Him. Was there any sorrow like

His sorrow?

Then there was the addition of some condiments.

Salt. "And every offering of your grain offering you shall season with salt; you shall not allow the salt of the covenant of your God to be lacking from your grain offering. With all your offerings you shall offer salt. . . . And you shall put oil on it, and lay frankincense on it. It is a grain offering" (Lev. 2:13, 15).

Salt holds many symbols. Two are referred to in verse 13: the salt of seasoning and the salt of the covenant. The salt of purification is not missing from the meaning of the verse. "And every offering of your grain offering you shall season with salt." This is the salt that brings out the true flavor of a thing so that it may be enjoyed to the full.

It has been observed that the leaven (corruption) had to be missing. Now the purity of the offering became more sure by the addition of salt, because salt is that which checks corruption and any form of putrefaction. It helps to maintain health.

". . . you shall not allow the salt of the covenant of your God to be lacking from your grain offering."

There were three covenants observed by the bedouin of the desert. They were the covenant of bread and wine, the covenant of salt, and the covenant of blood. The people of God were in the desert at this time and would be familiar with these things. God here introduced the second of these covenants, which established a relationship of friendship between bedouins. Additional references to this covenant of salt are to be found elsewhere in the Old

Testament. "All the heave offerings of the holy things, which the children of Israel offer to the Lord, I have given to you and your sons and daughters with you as an ordinance forever; it is a covenant of salt forever before the Lord with you and your descendants with you" (Num. 18:19). "Should you not know that the Lord God of Israel gave the dominion over Israel to David forever, to him and his sons, by a covenant of salt?" (2 Chron. 13:5).

The statement in Leviticus 2:13, therefore, means: "I present this gift because of the covenantal relationship in which I stand before Jehovah." This same thought is conveyed in the New Testament: "Let your speech always be with grace, seasoned with salt, that you may know how you ought to answer each one" (Col. 4:6). As Christians, we should so behave and conduct ourselves that we will be declaring to the world that we are a people who are in a covenant relationship with the Lord.

Frankincense. This is a spice that becomes effective through burning. It denoted prayer and intercession. A life work of effective service must be steeped in prayer. The most prayerful life spent on earth was that of the Lord Jesus Christ, who often spent whole nights in prayer. Fire caused the odor to rise, as trials, which drive us to our knees, cause our prayers to ascend to God.

The Offerer's Work—*Bring it to the priest.* "And he shall bring it to Aaron's sons, the priests" (Lev. 2:2).

Having prepared the offering as instructed, he now brought it to the priests and handed it over in its entirety. This was done at the door of the tabernacle. There was no ceremony, no participation, just a simple yieldedness, for there was nothing meritorious in his action, only obedience. In all the service we render to the Lord, none of it is to declare our worthiness, to display our merits, or to purchase our salvation. Service is a privilege, not a remuneration.

The Priest's Work—*Offer a handful.* He received the grain offering from the offerer, took from it a handful of the flour, grain, or cakes, with all the frankincense, and burned it on the altar. The remainder belonged to the priests. It was eaten by Aaron and his sons in the court of the tabernacle.

God's Portion—*The handful.* The handful of flour and all the frankincense were His. Only a small portion of this offering belonged to God, but it was a memorial—which means that the handful represented the whole in the sight of God and was accepted by Him as the whole.

Has it ever occurred to you that a very small portion of what we give to God, in both gifts and service, goes directly to Him? We give our tithes and our offerings, placing them in a collection plate or box. They become our gifts to God and yet they are taken and given to man—the minister's salary, the janitor's wages, the lighting and heating bills, the advertising, the repair and maintenance of the buildings. Other gifts go to missionary funds for fares, salaries, office staff, etc., until it appears that God receives nothing from our giving. But He does, inasmuch as He recognizes it, for by its means His work goes on.

Not only money but service can be self-centered. We spend much time in church activities, in making pictures and illustrations for children, in having clubs and outings for young people, in social events in the church, in hymn singing, choirs, solos, and instrumental ensembles—and a comparatively small portion of our time in actually teaching God's Word.

However, there is a handful which does belong exclusively to God, a portion in which man can have no part—that is, worship. May we, therefore, never become so active in service that we have no time for worship. "But the hour is coming, and now is, when the true worshipers will worship the Father in spirit and in truth; for the Father is seeking such to worship Him" (John 4:23).

The Priest's Portion—*The remainder*. All that remained after the handful had been removed. His time was occupied with the things of God. He had separated himself from the world to that end. The world contributes nothing to the support of the ministry; therefore the Church must. The Christian has a responsibility before God to provide what is necessary for the support of God's servants. God not only declared it but in His law He made provision for it. It is part of our service. Some of God's people are very generous in this respect, but others are more stingy in their relationship with God than they are with their friends. They will pay entrance fees for everything they want to see and enjoy but give nothing to the church from which they are receiving all of their spiritual food and their fellowship.

The priest had to partake of his portion within

the court of the tabernacle.

The Offerer's Portion—*Nothing*. God only accepts that which is wholeheartedly and willingly given. Ananias and Sapphira failed and perished because of a holding back that included deception. All our service must be done for the Lord with sincerity of heart. All the glory must be His also. The blessing becomes ours.

The Typical Teaching—*The kernel of wheat*. Each offering points to the Lord Jesus Christ and declares some attribute of that great offering made once at the end of that age. In the grain offering Christ is seen as the kernel of wheat which fell into the ground and died that He might bring forth much fruit. He was also the kernel of wheat which went through the crushing mill of Gethsemane and the fierce oven of Calvary to become the Bread of Life, the sustainer of His people on a pilgrim journey. He gave His all. He knew no reservation. He came not to be served but to serve and to give His life a ransom for many, and now upon Him we feed and in Him find our source of strength.

The Symbolism—*Consecration of gifts. Consecration of service*. The great truth to be noted is the order God has set forth. In the burnt offering it was the consecration of *self*. In the grain offering it was the consecration of *service*. And it is always in that order throughout Scripture. We cannot give our service until we have given ourselves, and when we have given ourselves we are then to give our service. Should these be placed in reverse order so that service comes first, we might find ourselves trying to give our service as a means of purchasing salvation—but this cannot be. Our works do not precede us for salvation, but our works do *follow* us. They have a place and they have reward. Hence we work out our salvation although we cannot work it in. The same truth is taught throughout the Word of God. In the New Testament the Lord said: "Therefore if you bring your gift to the altar, and there remember that your brother has something against you, leave your gift there before the altar, and go your way. First be reconciled to your brother, and then come and offer your gift" (Matt. 5:23–24)—reconciliation with the brother before presentation of gifts. God's requirement of man is reconciliation with Himself before the presentation of any gift or service.

Maybe the most beautiful illustration of this great truth has been lost in the fog of tradition. It belongs to the Christmas story and concerns the Wise Men who brought their gifts to the newborn King. The gifts brought on that occasion were actually four, and the most important one has been lost because we are ever speaking of and singing about the "three wise men from Orient far." They are seen everywhere on Christmas cards and in Christmas decorations, in church and commercial world alike. But from where have these *three* Wise Men come? Certainly not from the scriptural narrative, because that merely says: ". . . behold, wise men from the East came to Jerusalem, saying, 'Where is He who has been born King of the Jews? For we have seen His star in the East and have come to worship Him'" (Matt. 2:1–2). The number has been concluded from the number of gifts, but this conclusion is invalid because more than one person could carry either gold, frankincense, or myrrh.

According to protocol, when children are born to reigning monarchs all other kings, queens, and rulers of the world recognize these births by sending gifts. This is still done to the present day. When Jesus was born King of the Jews, protocol required that gifts should be sent. This is what these Wise Men were expected to do, but they did not. Instead of *sending* their gifts, they themselves took a long tedious journey across the desert on the backs of camels. "And when they had come into the house, they saw the young child with Mary His mother, and fell down, and worshiped Him. And when they had opened their treasures, they presented gifts to Him: gold, frankincense, and myrrh" (Matt. 2:11).

The very first gift they had offered was themselves. Instead of sending gifts by servants, they came and *fell down and worshiped*. It was an act of adoration, an act of humiliation, an act of surrender of themselves. After this most important surrender of self, they presented to Him their material gifts.

· Chapter 4 ·

The Sin Offering

Now the Lord spoke to Moses, saying, "Speak to the children of Israel, saying: 'If a person sins unintentionally against any of the commandments of the Lord in anything which ought not to be done, and does any of them, if the anointed priest sins, bringing guilt on the people, then let him offer to the Lord for his sin which he has sinned a young bull without blemish as a sin offering. He shall bring the bull to the door of the tabernacle of meeting before the Lord, lay his hand on the bull's head, and kill the bull before the Lord. Then the anointed priest shall take some of the bull's blood and bring it to the tabernacle of meeting. The priest shall dip his finger in the blood and sprinkle some of the blood seven times before the Lord, in front of the veil of the sanctuary. And the priest shall put some of the blood on the horns of the altar of sweet incense before the Lord, which is in the tabernacle of meeting; and he shall pour the remaining blood of the bull at the base of the altar of the burnt offering, which is at the door of the tabernacle of meeting. He shall take from it all the fat of the bull as the sin offering. The fat that covers the entrails, and all the fat which is on the entrails, the two kidneys, and the fat that is on them by the flanks, and the fatty lobe attached to the liver above the kidneys, he shall remove, as it was taken from the bull of the sacrifice of the peace offering; and the priest shall burn them on the altar of the burnt offering. But the bull's hide and all its flesh, with its head and legs, its entrails, and offal—the whole bull he shall carry outside the camp to a clean place, where the ashes are poured out, and burn it on wood with fire; where the ashes are poured out it shall be burned.

'Now if the whole congregation of Israel sins unintentionally, and the thing is hidden from the eyes of the assembly, and they have done something against any of the commandments of the Lord in anything which should not be done, and are guilty; when the sin which they have sinned becomes known, then the assembly shall offer a young bull for the sin, and bring it before the tabernacle of meeting. And the elders of the congregation shall lay their hands on the head of the bull before the Lord. Then the bull shall be killed before the Lord. The anointed priest shall bring some of the bull's blood to the tabernacle of meeting. Then the priest shall dip his finger in the blood, and sprinkle it seven times before the Lord, in front of the veil. And he shall put some of the blood on the horns of the altar which is before the Lord, which is in the tabernacle of meeting; and he shall pour the remaining blood at the base of the altar of the burnt offering, which is at the door of the tabernacle of meeting. He shall take all the fat from it and burn it on the altar. And he shall do with the bull as he did with the bull as a sin offering; thus he shall do with it. So the priest shall make atonement for them, and it shall be forgiven them. Then he shall carry the bull outside the camp, and burn it as he burned the first bull. It is a sin offering for the assembly.

'When a ruler has sinned, and done something unintentionally against any of the commandments of the Lord his God in anything which should not be done, and is guilty, or if his sin which he has sinned comes to his knowledge, he shall bring as his offering a kid of the goats, a male without blemish. And he shall lay his hand on the head of the goat, and kill it at the place where they kill the burnt offering before the Lord. It is a sin offering. The priest shall take some of the blood of the sin offering with his finger, put it on the horns of the altar of burnt offering, and pour its blood at the base of the altar of burnt offering. And he shall burn all its fat on the altar, like the fat of the sacrifice of peace offering. So the priest shall make atonement for him concerning his sin, and it shall be forgiven him.

'If anyone of the common people sins unintentionally by doing something against any of the commandments of the Lord in anything which ought not to be done, and is guilty, or if his sin which he has sinned comes to his knowledge, then he shall bring as his offering a kid of the goats, a female without blemish, for his sin which he has sinned. And he shall lay his hand on the head of the sin offering, and kill the sin offering in the place of the burnt offering. Then the priest shall take some of its blood with his finger, and put it on the horns of the altar of burnt offering, and pour its remaining blood at the base of the altar. He shall remove all its fat, as fat is removed from the sacrifice of peace offering; and the priest shall burn it on the altar for a sweet aroma to the Lord. So the priest shall make atonement for him, and it shall be forgiven him.

'If he brings a lamb as his sin offering, he shall bring a female without blemish. Then he shall lay his hand on the head of the sin offering, and slay it as a sin offering at the place where they kill the burnt offering. The priest shall take some of the blood of the sin offering with his finger, put it on the horns of the altar of burnt offering, and pour its remaining blood at the base of the altar. He shall remove all its fat, as the fat of the lamb is removed from the sacrifice of the peace offering. Then the priest shall burn it upon the altar, according to the offerings made by fire to the Lord. So the priest shall make atonement for his sin that he has committed, and it shall be forgiven him.'" (Lev. 4:1–35)

And the Lord spoke to Moses, saying, "Speak to Aaron and to his sons, saying, 'This is the law of the sin offering: In the place where the burnt offering is killed, the sin offering shall be killed before the Lord. It is most holy. The priest who offers it for sin shall eat it. In a holy place it shall be eaten, in the court of the tabernacle of meeting. Everyone who touches its flesh must be holy. And when its blood is sprinkled on any garment, you shall wash that on which it was sprinkled, in a holy place. But the earthen vessel in which it is boiled shall be broken. And if it is boiled in a bronze pot, it shall be both scoured and rinsed in water. All the males among the priests may eat it. It is most holy. But no sin offering from which any of the blood is brought into the tabernacle of meeting, to make atonement in the holy place, shall be eaten. It shall be burned in the fire.'" (Lev. 6:24–30)

IT HAS ALREADY been pointed out that the peace offering was last in the list of observances but third in the classification of these Levitical chapters. In these studies it is being placed last. Therefore, the sin offering is now to be considered. This is the first of the two compulsory offerings.

The Nature of the Offering—*According to position. Bull, goat, or lamb.* These differed from the animals of the burnt offerings in that there were no birds. The variation of the animals in this offering was . . .

According to position. These are designated:

(1) *Priest.* "If the anointed priest sins, bringing guilt on the people, then let him offer to the Lord for his sin which he has sinned a young bull without blemish as a sin offering" (Lev. 4:3).

(2) *Whole congregation.* "Now if the whole congregation of Israel sins unintentionally . . . when the sin which they have sinned becomes known, then the assembly shall offer a young bull for the sin, and bring it before the tabernacle of meeting" (Lev. 4:13–14).

(3) *Ruler.* "When a ruler has sinned, and done something unintentionally against any of the commandments of the Lord his God in anything which should not be done, and is guilty . . . he shall bring as his offering a kid of the goats, a male without blemish" (Lev. 4:22–23).

(4) *Commoner.* "And if anyone of the common people sins unintentionally . . . then he shall bring as his offering a kid of the goats, a female without blemish, for his sin which he has sinned" (Lev. 4:27–28).

In these classifications it is to be seen that:

A priest offered a young bull.

The whole congregation offered a young bull.

The ruler offered a young male goat.

The commoner offered a young female goat.

The offerings required by God for the priest and the whole congregation were equal, or, in the sight of God, the sin of a priest was as great as the sin of a whole congregation, because if a man in an official capacity sins, he can lead a whole nation astray. It was John Trapp, one of the old divines, who said: "If a teacher sins he teaches sin." High position means high responsibility. If you are a pastor, a teacher, a Bible class leader, a deacon; if you hold any church office, then you need to be especially careful in your conduct because others are taking you as an example.

The offering of a ruler was a *male* kid, a symbol of authority, but for a commoner, who had no authority, the offering was a female. In each instance the sacrifice needed to be perfect, without blemish, because it foreshadowed the perfect Sacrifice. The difference lay in the treatment of the blood and in the disposition of the carcass.

Four times, "unintentionally" is repeated. Responsibility is not pushed aside very easily. In our civil laws, the powers that be seldom seem to listen to our pleas of ignorance. If we have broken the law we pay the price. How much more with God! Ignorance is not easily established; much of the ignorance we seek to claim is willful. We could have found out the facts but we did not bother.

The Offerer's Work—*Identify himself. To slay the sacrifice.* This offering was to be made at the gate of the tabernacle court, the place of God's choosing. God did not permit this sacrifice for sin to be made just anywhere. This would have led to uncontrolled practices, idolatry, the establishment of sacred sites. In fact, all these things are with us today. The cross is being replaced by ceremonial practices. The church, as an organism, is being substituted by organization. The Bible is being pushed aside for creeds and credentials.

The offerer then placed his hands firmly upon

the head of the animal. In the case of the whole
nation having sinned, this would be done by the
elders, who would be their representatives. This act
had a twofold significance. In the first place, it was
one of identification. They identified themselves as
one with the animal that was about to die, just as by
the act of placing our thumb impression upon a document we identify ourselves with that document. Secondly, it was an act of imputation. They believed
that their sins passed from them to the animal, so
that, when it died, it died in their place.

The offerer then slew the animal. He was the
one who had sinned; therefore he was the one responsible for the death of the animal. It is easy to
blame the Jewish nation for the death of Jesus. Likewise, anyone can lay the charge against Pilate who
condemned, or the Roman soldiers who crucified
Jesus. But, in reality, it was *our* sins that nailed Him
to the tree.

The Priest's Work—*Sprinkling blood.* He took the
blood of the sin offering into the Holy Place and
sprinkled it seven times before the Lord, before the
veil of the sanctuary. This signified God's acceptance. After this, as he came out, he applied the
blood here and there. The order is beautifully set
forth—before the Lord, in front of the veil, on the
horns of the altar of incense, at the brazen altar of
sacrifice where the remainder was poured out.

The picture is that of the blood being applied as
he came out, not as he went in. Salvation is of the
Lord. The way was opened from God to man. It was
opened by our great High Priest, the Lord Jesus Christ.

It was opened through the shedding of His blood, and along that bloodstained way man travels from outside to within. We meet Christ at Calvary, where He poured out His soul as the offering for sin; then we proceed to the golden altar, the place of His intercession, and on to the veil now rent, giving us access into the presence of the eternal God—in whose presence we stand perfect in Christ.

In the event of the offering being that of a ruler or commoner, the blood remained outside.

The priest then took all the fat of the innards and burned it on the altar (the significance of the fat will be found in Chapter 6 concerning the peace offering).

Having dealt with the blood, then came the disposal of the carcass. This must have seemed extraordinary to the priest who had to take the whole of it and carry it outside the camp to the place where he poured the ashes. There were very strict conditions under which it was carried out. "But the bull's hide and all its flesh, with its head and legs, its entrails and offal—the whole bull he shall carry outside the camp to a clean place, where the ashes are poured out, and burn it on wood with fire; where the ashes are poured out it shall be burned" (Lev. 4:11–12). "But no sin offering from which any of the blood is brought into the tabernacle of meeting, to make atonement in the holy place, shall be eaten. It shall be burned in the fire" (Lev. 6:30).

All this was ordained by God because He intended them to understand the severity of His judgment on sin. Sin was now in this animal by reason of imputation, so it must be carried away carefully and destroyed totally. This was known as . . .

God's Portion—*The whole*. No part of this animal was for man. No part of it could be used as food. We live in a day when we have lost the sense of the holiness of God, His sovereignty, and His severity. All the judgment of our sin fell upon the Son of His love when He, who knew no sin, became sin and died in our place. This price that was paid cost God the very best that He had—His Only Begotten Son, He who was in the bosom of the Father in a past eternity. No wonder there is no mercy for sin outside of Christ's redeeming work!

Yet, despite all these things, part of the sacrifice did become . . .

The Priest's Portion—*Part of the commoner's*. The priest was always rewarded for the service rendered. However, his part came from the offering of the ruler or commoner, never part of the priest's or the congregation's, because he himself could be a partaker of such sins. He had a share of the sheep or goat, but never of the bull. We gather this from the fact that the carcass of the sheep or goat was not carried outside. "The priest who offers it for sin shall eat it. In a holy place it shall be eaten, in the court of the tabernacle of meeting" (Lev. 6:26). Even so, the vessels used for boiling had to be destroyed. "But the earthen vessel in which it is boiled shall be broken. and if it is boiled in a bronze pot, it shall be both scoured and rinsed in water" (Lev. 6:28).

The Offerer's Portion—*Nothing*. This was the sin offering, and we are the guilty party. We can do

nothing at all in the matter of our sin or our redemption. It is all of grace.

The Typical Teaching—*Christ is our Sin Offering*. The priest may sin, nations may fall into idolatry, rulers may lead people astray, individuals may
fail and come short—for *all* have sinned and fall
short of the glory of God. Whoever, wherever, however, sin is sin; whether we call it small or large,
black or white, justifiable or unjustifiable, intentional
or unintentional, it makes no difference so far as
God is concerned. It must be dealt with, and He
Himself has made the complete and only provision,
which is declared in the New Testament: "For what
the law could not do in that it was weak through the
flesh, God did by sending His own Son in the likeness of sinful flesh, on account of sin: He condemned
sin in the flesh" (Rom. 8:3).

To understand this verse, one or two questions
must be asked—the first, What was it that the law
could not do? The psalmist says: "The law of the
Lord is perfect, converting the soul" (Ps. 19:7). The
answer is given in Galatians 2:16: "Knowing that a
man is not justified by the works of the law but by
faith in Jesus Christ, even we have believed in Christ
Jesus, that we might be justified by faith in Christ,
and not by the works of the law; for by the works of
the law no flesh shall be justified." The law could
not justify. It covered sin but was unable to remove
the sin.

The second question would be, If the law was
made weak through the flesh, then what sort of flesh?
It is generally assumed that this refers to the human

flesh or our sinful flesh, but this interpretation does not fit into the text. Human flesh cannot weaken a perfect or eternal law. There is a better explanation.

The law required that when a man sinned he should offer a young animal as a sin offering. But how could an animal take the place of a sinner and bring him deliverance from sin? Man is human, the sacrifice is animal. Man is a moral being, the animal is amoral. They are of two different natures. Man knows temptation, trial, failure, sin; but the animal knows none of these things. It has no moral standards, knows no law, has no sense of right and wrong; in other words, it does not possess my flesh, my nature, my morals. It is totally different in its being; therefore, how could it take my place and become my substitute? The answer is that it could not. So the law, with its demands, became weak or noneffective through the flesh of that animal. Therefore ". . . what the law could not do [justify] in that it was weak through the flesh [animal flesh], God did by sending His own Son in the likeness of sinful flesh [human flesh—Jesus becoming Man], on account of sin: He condemned sin in the flesh" (Rom. 8:3). "For He made Him who knew no sin to be sin for us, that we might become the righteousness of God in Him" (2 Cor. 5:21).

As in this offering sin passed from man to the sinless animal by the laying on of hands (imputation), after which the animal was slain (expiation)— so by faith my sin passed from me, the sinful one, to Christ, the sinless One, causing Him to become my sin. Then, when He died, my sin died in Him and I live, having been made the righteousness of God in Him.

A third New Testament passage bearing on this same subject is: "We have an altar from which those who serve the tabernacle have no right to eat. For the bodies of those beasts, whose blood is brought into the sanctuary by the high priest for sin, are burned outside the camp. Therefore Jesus also, that He might sanctify the people with His own blood, suffered outside the gate. Therefore let us go forth to Him, outside the camp, bearing His reproach" (Heb. 13:10–13).

Two things stand out prominently in these verses. The blood went in—the body went out. The body went outside the camp in judgment because sin was on it. The blood went in, in reconciliation, because God had accepted it. Outside, Christ met man's need; inside, Christ met God's demands, and so a reconciliation was made. If we are identified with Him in His suffering in the world today, we shall be welcomed together with Him in His glory by and by.

The Symbolism—*Atonement.* So far as we are concerned . . .

> Jesus paid it all,
> All to Him I owe;
> Sin had left a crimson stain,
> He washed it white as snow.

Death has taken place; the price has been paid. We are free through expiation.

· Chapter 5 ·

The Trespass Offering

"And he shall bring his trespass offering to the Lord for his sin which he has sinned, a female from the flock, a lamb or a kid of the goats as a sin offering. So the priest shall make atonement for him concerning his sin. If he is not able to bring a lamb, then he shall bring to the Lord, for his trespass which he has committed, two turtledoves or two young pigeons: one as a sin offering and the other as a burnt offering." (Lev. 5:6–7)

"Likewise this is the law of the trespass offering (it is most holy): In the place where they killed the burnt offering they shall kill the trespass offering. And its blood he shall sprinkle all around on the altar. And he shall offer from it all its fat. The fat tail and the fat that covers the entrails, the two kidneys, and the fat that on them by the flanks, and the fatty lobe attached to the liver above the kidneys, he shall remove; and the priest shall burn them on the altar as an offering made by fire to the Lord. It is a trespass offering. Every male among the priests may eat it. It shall be eaten in a holy place. It is most holy.

"The trespass offering is like the sin offering; there is one law for them both: the priest who makes atonement with it shall have it. And the priest who offers anyone's burnt offering, that priest shall have for himself the skin of the burnt offering which he has offered. Also every grain offering that is baked in the oven and all that is prepared in the covered pan, or in a pan, shall be the priest's who offers it. Every grain offering mixed with oil, or dry, shall belong to all the sons of Aaron, to one as much as the other." (Lev. 7:1–10)

THE TRESPASS offering—called the "guilt offering" in some other translations—will have to be approached differently from the others because, in this instance, the offering was . . .

According to practice. It was applicable to a number of specific sins which were important enough to be listed by God, and so are important enough to demand our individual attention. One of the notable distinctions between the sin offering and the trespass offering is that in the latter, restitution was always required. Of course, the trespass offering was in fact part of the sin offering. Sin is coming short of God's standards. Trespassing is overstepping the mark. It also means the unlawful possession or use of another's property. We see this in the common notice: "Trespassers will be prosecuted." A boundary line is involved.

The Trespass. We shall now take a look at ten specific trespasses listed in the book of Leviticus.

(1) *Concealing truth.* "If a person sins in hearing the utterance of an oath, and is a witness, whether he has seen or known of the matter—if he does not tell it, he bears guilt" (Lev. 5:1).

The object of this divine command is to keep crime in check, and also to protect the innocent. In view of this, any person who withholds evidence when it is demanded in the name of justice becomes a participant in the crime. This is known in British and American law as "aiding and abetting," and is punishable. History is full of evidence to this fact. This is why in the law courts a person is required to take an oath on the Bible to "declare the truth, the whole truth, and nothing but the truth." If we are to live honorably before God we must live honestly before men.

Two examples of this law, from the Old and New Testaments, one negative and the other positive, are worthy of our attention.

After Joshua destroyed the city of Jericho and moved on to the smaller town of Ai, the Israelites were defeated. The reason was revealed: sin was in the camp. Achan had stolen some of the spoils of Jericho, which were to have been dedicated to the Lord. When this was discovered, he and his sons and daughters were stoned to death. Some people have had a problem with why his family should have died because of the sin of their father. The inference is that the family was aware of the sin and had not made it known, so that when—by a process of elimination—Achan was discovered, the children were participants in the sin by their silence.

The more outstanding and positive illustration comes from the life of the Lord. Jesus was standing before the false witnesses who were accusing Him of many things, to which the Lord made no response. This so angered the high priest that he cried: "Do you answer nothing? What is it that these men testify against you?" (Matt. 26:62). But Jesus kept silent. The Lord was certainly fulfilling the prophecy Isaiah had made concerning Him: "He was oppressed and He was afflicted, yet He opened not His mouth;

He was led as a lamb to the slaughter, and as a sheep before its shearers is dumb, so He opened not His mouth" (Isa. 53:7).

Caiaphas, indignant with his "prisoner" (and, as high priest, fully acquainted with the law), made use of Leviticus 5:1 when he said: "I adjure you by the living God that you tell us if you are the Christ, the Son of God" (Matt. 26:63). Jesus had now been charged to answer under oath. If, at that moment, He had failed to answer, He would have committed a sin, become a sinner, and failed to become man's Redeemer. However, Jesus was as fully cognizant of the law as was Caiaphas, and replied: "It is as you said" (Matt. 26:64), and thereby remained sinless.

A Christian ought to live as consistently as this every day.

(2) *Defilement*. "Or if a person touches any unclean thing . . . or if he touches human uncleanness . . . when he realizes it, then he shall be guilty" (Lev. 5:2–3).

This sounds like a harsh law, but one must remember that the children of Israel were surrounded by nations steeped in idolatry, and God was concerned that His people should keep themselves from being contaminated with what would defile not only the body but also the soul. God was seeking to reach the spiritual life of His people through the medium of material things. A dead body or a leprous person would defile anyone who contacted it, just as in the present there are certain diseases known to be contagious, and therefore every precaution is taken to avoid such. The Lord's aim is to teach us to shun as sin every form of impurity—whether it be through sight or conversation or acquaintance—for such things can defile our soul and damage our spiritual life. Even if one does these things in ignorance and learns of it later, he is guilty.

(3) *Swearing rashly.* "Or if a person swears, speaking thoughtlessly with his lips to do evil or to do good, whatever it is that a man may pronounce by an oath, and it is hidden from him—when he realizes it, then he shall be guilty in any of these matters" (Lev. 5:4).

This is very different from the act of swearing under oath. It is related to making promises, entering into contracts, or making vows.

On reading the verse, again it would appear that there is an outstanding injustice, if not a contradiction. It is understandable that if a person declared that he would perform some good thing and then failed to do it, he would be in the wrong. But if a person declared that he was going to carry out some evil project and then repented of his intent, surely that change would be justifiable! But the text says no. He is still a guilty man.

This is a matter of emphasis. The verse is not concerned with the good or the evil; it is concerned with the oath. It is a demand for care in the form of our speech, which can quickly cause us to fall into sin. Our promises to do good or evil must not be rash, and they must never be taken in the name of the Lord. So often people promise to give money, maintain a missionary, give this or do that, in the name of the Lord. Often one is asked to sign a pledge of some kind—"I promise by the help of God." This is a thing that the Lord does not encourage, because "you shall not take the name of the Lord your God in vain, for the Lord will not hold him guiltless who takes His name in vain" (Exod. 20:7). To promise anything in the name of the Lord and then fail in its fulfillment is to take His name in vain. It is "swearing rashly." Never bring that holy name of the Lord into the affairs of life unless you are determined that at *all* costs you will fulfill that commitment.

Here is what the Word of the Lord has to say about it: "Again you have heard that it was said to those of old, 'You shalt not swear falsely, but shall perform your oaths to the Lord.' But I say to you, do not swear at all: neither by heaven, for it is God's throne; nor by the earth, for it is His footstool; nor by Jerusalem, for it is the city of the great King. Nor shall you swear by your head, because you cannot make one hair white or black. But let your 'Yes' be 'Yes,' and your 'No,' 'No.' For whatever is more than these is from the evil one" (Matt. 5:33–37). "But above all, my brethren, do not swear, either by heaven or by earth or with any other oath. But let your 'Yes' be 'Yes,' and your 'No,' 'No,' lest you fall into judgment" (James 5:12). Therefore, in all promises just be satisfied with a yes or no.

The psalmist also warned us about careful use of our words when he said: "Set a guard, O Lord, over my mouth; keep watch over the door of my lips" (Ps. 141:3).

Jacob, when he fled from Esau his brother, was met by God at Bethel. In his alarm "Jacob made a vow, saying, 'If God will be with me, and keep me in this way that I am going, and give me bread to eat and clothing to put on, so that I come back to my father's house in peace, then the Lord shall be my God. And this stone which I have set as a pillar shall be God's house, and of all that You give me I will surely give a tenth to You" (Gen. 28:20–22).

God, who often referred to Himself as "the God of Abraham, of Isaac, and of Jacob," appeared to Jacob and said: "I am the God of Bethel, where you anointed the pillar and where you made a vow to me. Now arise, get out of this land, and return to the land of your kindred" (Gen. 31:13).

Many people have been perplexed concerning the story of Jephthah and cannot accept that he offered his daughter as a sacrifice. (And it is a harsh story.) Therefore they explain that she lived a life of virginity—their reasoning being that God did not permit human sacrifice. This is true, but neither does God allow His name to be taken in vain. The heart of the story is: "And Jephthah made a vow to the Lord, and said, 'If You will indeed deliver the people of Ammon into my hands, then it will be that whatever comes out of the doors of my house to meet me . . . I will offer it up as a burnt offering.'" (Read Judges 11:29–40.) Better to offer a human sacrifice than profane the name of a holy God.

All this is borne out by yet another Scripture passage: "If a man vows a vow to the Lord, or swears an oath to bind himself by some agreement, he shall not break his word; he shall do according to all that proceeds out of his mouth. Or if a woman vows a vow to the Lord, and binds herself by some agreement while in her father's house in her youth, and her father hears her vow and the agreement by which she has bound herself, and her father holds his peace, then all her vows shall stand, and every agreement with which she has bound herself shall stand" (Num. 30:2–4).

Humbleness and gentleness are the safest paths of life, letting our yes be yes, and our no, no—which mean yes or no without the addition of oaths and promises that become committals that bind. God binds the man who binds himself with an oath.

Special note must be made of the fact that if the oath were *good* and the man failed to fulfill it, he was guilty and must offer a trespass offering. If a man swore to do *evil* and he did not do it, he sinned. This man was in a dilemma. If he did the thing he declared, he sinned. If he did not commit the act, he still sinned and must offer his trespass offering—which means that in the mind of God breaking a vow is more grievous than fulfilling an evil intent, so the lesser must be done because of the import of the greater. In the light of this, let us pray: "Lord, guard Thou the words of my lips."

(4) *Dishonesty in holy things.* "If a person commits a trespass, and sins unintentionally in regard to the holy things of the Lord, then he shall bring to the Lord as his trespass offering a ram without blemish from the flocks, with your valuation in shekels of silver according to the shekel of the sanctuary, as a trespass offering. And he shall make restitution for the harm that he has done in regard to the holy

thing, and shall add the one-fifth to it and give it to the priest. So the priest shall make atonement for him with the ram of the trespass offering, and it shall be forgiven him" (Lev. 5:15–16).

Dishonesty is twofold. It can be against God or it can be against man. In these immediate verses, and in those that follow concerning ignorance, the sins were against God. The remaining details of the trespass offering were sins against man.

Man might be as free today as he was in the days of Malachi to ask if it were possible for a man to rob God, and the answer would still be the same—yes, even though it might be through ignorance in his understanding of holy things.

We must remember that everything belongs to God, and man, too, belongs to Him, for He is the creator and the sustainer of all things. He is the sovereign ruler of the earth. "All things were made through Him, and without Him nothing was made that was made" (John 1:3).

God claimed for Himself the firstborn of man and animal (Exod. 13:2).

God claimed half a shekel per head ransom money from every man who joined the army of Israel (Exod. 30:11–16).

God claimed the firstfruits of the harvest (Lev. 23:10–14).

God claimed tithes of all man possessed—and that would include time, energy, and service, as well as possessions (Lev. 27:30–32).

When God gave Israel the land of promise, as they entered into its conquest under the leadership of Joshua, He required that the first city, Jericho, should be dedicated to Himself by fire (Josh. 6).

In the New Testament He has claimed much more because He has given to man much more. He gave Himself; He asks that we should give ourselves. But man has always been slow to give to God the things He requests—even more: the things He demands. To withhold is to rob. "Will a man rob God? Yet you have robbed Me! But you say, 'In what way have we robbed You?' In tithes and offerings" (Mal. 3:8). It may be unintentional, but that does not alter man's responsibility.

God is robbed when we fail to give Him that one day in seven for worship and quiet meditation. He has given us six days and asks that we should give Him one. Is He asking too much? As a nation we have robbed Him of that day and can no longer expect His blessing. But how about ourselves as individuals—do we rob God?

God is robbed in our defective liberality. "Bring all the tithes into the storehouse" (Mal. 3:10). God is robbed in our lack of responsibility toward the Christian ministry, for He has declared that a laborer is worthy of his hire. God is robbed in our failure to maintain His work. The church is yielding ground everywhere because of lack of support financially and in practical ways. We are not supporting God's church by our presence at the meetings, by our prayers for the ministry, by our interest in the missionary program, by our personal invitation to others, as it ought to be supported. God is robbed of the worship due to His holy name. He is robbed when we neglect His Word. What we do today amounts to a constant asking of favors from God without giving worship to our God.

Are we honest with our time, our possessions, our abilities, our privileges, our responsibilities, our friends?

This dishonesty in holy things is a trespass for which God requires amends and restoration.

(5) *Ignorance.* "If a person sins, and commits any of these things which are forbidden to be done by the commandments of the Lord, though he does not know it, yet he is guilty and shall bear his iniquity" (Lev. 5:17).

The sin of ignorance is not only stated in the above verse but is repeated a number of times in the chapter in the words "though he does not know it" or "and it is hidden from him." On first reading this would appear to be another injustice, but on second reading—upon consideration—we should realize that it is not so. The natural man reasons that if he is ignorant, how can he be responsible?

The author remembers reasoning with the police on one occasion when his car had been impounded because, ignorantly, it had been parked in a non-parking area. All the pleading of innocence was of no avail. Sin, known or unknown, is a departure from the right. ". . . where there is no law there is no transgression" (Rom. 4:15). But we are not without law. The problem was that the police had set up a signpost indicating the new law, but I had not seen it because of an obstruction. Although I did not know it, the law had still been broken and so guilt was established.

The questions to be asked are, Why are we ignorant? Is the claim of ignorance just? Much of what we claim to be ignorance is willful and therefore is sin. If a local authority provides motorists with a manual of rules and conduct on the highway, and the motorist refuses or does not bother to read the manual, can he claim ignorance? The law says no. Such a person is punishable, and the rest of society would agree.

God has provided mankind with a manual of laws and conduct—the Bible. In it God has laid down His laws. He has set forth the whole code for a moral life and all the principles of a spiritual life. He has declared the punishments that must be meted out for disobedience and the rewards for obedience. If a man refuses to read the Bible to find the mind of God, or, having read it fails to accept its revelation or satisfies himself with his own interpretation of that law—accepting this and rejecting that— then he becomes guilty in the eyes of God. This man is definitely willful. If a man could find out but does not, he is guilty. Needless forgetfulness is also sin. This is not ignorance; it is the sin of ignorance.

Blunting spiritual perception is willful ignorance. Measuring conduct by our own standards is willful.

If the Jews had read their law with an open mind, they would have known their Messiah. Then they would not have crucified the Lord of glory. If one does not know, then it becomes his duty to find out.

The next trespasses named were not against God but against our fellow man.

(6) *Failure in our trust.* "If a person sins and commits a trespass against the Lord by lying to his neighbor about what was delivered to him for safekeeping . . ." (Lev. 6:2).

If one accepts another person's property or possessions, with the promise to protect or safeguard them, he becomes morally responsible to fulfill the promise and in due time to return to the owner that which has been in his custody. To accept the possession with an ulterior motive, or to fail to secure it so that it cannot be lost or stolen, is a "lie." To make an excuse to the owner to deliver oneself from the responsibility accepted is also a "lie." The lesson to learn here is that we are required to be responsible people and that every commitment in life is very important. Again it is the matter of honesty—in 2 Kings 6:5 it is recorded: "But as one was cutting down a tree, the iron ax head fell into the water; and he cried out and said, 'Alas, master! for it was borrowed.'" The concern was that the ax was not his, it was borrowed. Man must be concerned about borrowed goods, and even more concerned about entrusted goods. May the Lord deliver us from carelessness at any time, because we will be held responsible for such conduct and will have to make amends—such is trespassing.

(7) *Unfairness in partnership.* "If a person sins and commits a trespass against the Lord . . . about a pledge" (Lev. 6:2).

Another translation of the word "pledge" is "contract." The idea is one of partnership. The Lord is showing what His mind is concerning our everyday behavior as people who are in the world but not of it. How do we relate to other people? Is that relationship such as is worthy of the gospel of Jesus Christ and our Christian profession?

This partnership not only operates in the business world, where we are not to be unequally yoked with unbelievers, but it applies in all ways and in all things where another person is involved. It is doing the fair share, not acting as top dog and taking the choice parts, always being the leader and letting the other person do the dirty work or carry the heavy load. This applies in business, in the home, in the church, in our social life, everywhere—always playing a fair game.

(8) *Taking by violence.* "If a person sins and commits a trespass against the Lord . . . about a robbery" (Lev. 6:2).

This statement is not limited to open assault, hitting and robbing somebody on the highway. A Christian would not even think of doing such a thing. It is that each individual has a will, and that will is as much his as is his money or any other material possession. Everyone has a right to think. He is entitled to make his own decisions and conduct himself as his conscience permits.

There are strong-willed, determined people who insist on having their own way and exercising their authority, or their thinking, irrespective of whether their neighbor agrees or whether his conscience is hurt or offended. This is taking the other man's personality and mind from him by violence. The dictionary says, among other things, that violence is "any unjust or unwarranted exertion of force or power, as against rights, laws, etc." As Christians we need to learn to respect other persons' rights and privileges. We may try to persuade someone to change his point of view, but never should we force him. We must learn to agree, or to agree to differ.

(9) *Deception.* "If a person sins and commits a trespass against the Lord . . . or if he has extorted from his neighbor" (Lev. 6:2).

This means to obtain under false pretenses—to defraud or cheat. The Bible is full of records of deception and the consequences. Jacob deceived Esau, the Gibeonites deceived Joshua, Delilah deceived Samson, Ananias and Sapphira sought to deceive Peter. Today children deceive their parents and teachers, workmen deceive their masters and masters their workpeople. Even Christians deceive each other, and many of us try to deceive God. In the sight of God these are trespasses against each other for which we will be held responsible and for which God demands amends.

(10) *Keeping things found.* "If a person sins and commits a trespass against the Lord . . . or he has found what was lost and lies concerning it, and swears falsely" (Lev. 6:2–3).

This is a dishonesty. As Christians it is our duty to do all that is within our power to discover the owner of anything we may find and see that it is duly returned. "Finders, keepers" is a worldly attitude that is both selfish and wrong. The Lord has always required absolute honesty.

Having detailed the practices, the ritual of this

trespass offering must now be considered.

The Nature of the Offering—*According to practice. Lamb, goat, turtledoves, pigeons, fine flour.* In the first three failures, the offering was a female lamb or a kid of the goats, or two turtledoves or two young pigeons, all of them in the prime of life. This offering included a sin offering and a burnt offering. Some scholars consider that the first fifteen verses of chapter five are still the sin offering. It is a little difficult to discern because, on the one hand, the word trespass is used, while, on the other hand, part of the sin offering was required. However, there was the alternative of one-tenth of an ephah of fine flour that could be offered (vs. 11), and this would not have met the requirements of the sin offering.

In the rest of the failures the situation is a little clearer. A ram was included, plus an estimation, plus a fine equal to a double tithe—two-tenths or one-fifth. When the trespass was against man there was the restoration of the principal, plus a fifth, to the owner, and a ram, with a fine, to the priest.

One of the major differences between the sin offering and the trespass offering was that in the latter restitution was always required.

The Offerer's Work—*Confession.* "And it shall be, when he is guilty in any of these matters, that he shall confess that he has sinned in that thing" (Lev. 5:5). "Then it shall be, because he has sinned and is guilty, that . . . he shall restore its full value, add one-fifth more to it, and give it to whomever it belongs, on the day of his trespass offering" (Lev. 6:4–5).

First, the offerer had to make confession *"in that*

thing." This was not a general confession which could be an easy ritualistic citation. It was a personal, particular confession of a specific sin committed. This brought about a deep sense of guilt, followed by humiliation. He must obtain forgiveness and must make restitution, plus that which again emphasized guilt, thus making sin and carelessness to be unprofitable matters.

Present-day crime could be greatly reduced, and innocent people protected, if our prevailing laws were based upon those laid down by God, so that crime became expensive to the criminal instead of lucrative.

The Priest's Work—*Sprinkling blood.* In the matter of the first three trespasses, the blood of the first bird was sprinkled on the side of the altar and the remainder of the blood poured out at the bottom of the altar. The second bird was used as a burnt offering. In the event of the offering being one of fine flour, a handful was burned by the priest as it was given to God. In the remaining trespasses, the blood of the ram was sprinkled around the altar, as in the sin offering—without the shedding of blood there is no remission.

God's Portion—*All that was burned.* This was the rump and all the internal fat. The fat was the best because of its significance (see God's portion of the peace offering).

The Priest's Portion—*The remainder.* That which was not offered to God by fire. The portion which went to God was always a memorial—that which represented and was accepted as the whole. The servants of God are sharers in the blessings of God.

The Offerer's Portion—*Nothing*. He was the offender and was meeting the requirements of the law. As an offender he had no merits.

The Typical Teaching—*Christ our Trespass Offering*. "For the transgressions of My people He was stricken" (Isa. 53:8).

Christ has given Himself, the one offering for sin, and He died. We are all debtors to God, having trespassed against Him; but since we are unable to pay the penalty required by law, He became the lamb, the goat, the turtledove, the young pigeon, even the fine flour, and so has made full provision. Hence the claims of God were not avoided but justly met in Him who was our Trespass Offering. ". . . God was in Christ reconciling the world to Himself, not imputing their trespasses to them, and has committed to us the word of reconciliation" (2 Cor. 5:19). "And you, being dead in your trespasses and the uncircumcision of your flesh, He has made alive together with Him, having forgiven you all trespasses, having wiped out the handwriting of requirements that was against us, which was contrary to us. And He has taken it out of the way, having nailed it to the cross" (Col. 2:13–14).

Symbolism—*Restoration*. While the Lord has made full provision for us with the Father, we have certain commitments and responsibilities here on earth. The trespasser had in each instance to make amends, restoring all his wrongful gains. Lest some might want to see something meritorious in simply "making good," a confession of the wrong he had done had to be made, and a sacrifice had to go with it as a token of complete unworthiness.

· CHAPTER 6 ·

The Peace Offering

"When his offering is a sacrifice of peace offering, if he offers it of the herd, whether male or female, he shall offer it without blemish before the Lord. And he shall lay his hand on the head of his offering, and kill it at the door of the tabernacle of meeting; and Aaron's sons, the priests, shall sprinkle the blood all around on the altar. Then he shall offer from the sacrifice of the peace offering an offering made by fire to the Lord. The fat that covers the entrails and all the fat that is on the entrails, the two kidneys and the fat that is on them by the flanks, and the fatty lobe attached to the liver above the kidneys, he shall remove; and Aaron's sons shall burn it on the altar upon the burnt sacrifice, which is on the wood that is on the fire, as an offering made by fire, a sweet aroma to the Lord.

"If his offering as a sacrifice of peace offering to the Lord is of the flock, whether male or female, he shall offer it without blemish. If he offers a lamb as his offering, then he shall offer it before the Lord. And he shall lay his hand on the head of his offering, and kill it before the tabernacle of meeting; and Aaron's sons shall sprinkle its blood all around on the altar. Then he shall offer from the sacrifice of the peace offering, as an offering made by fire to the Lord, its fat and the whole fat tail which he shall remove close to the backbone. And the fat that covers the entrails and all the fat that is on the entrails, the two kidneys, and the fat that is on them by the flanks, and the fatty lobe attached to the liver above the kidneys, he shall remove; and the priest shall burn them on the altar as food, an offering made by fire to the Lord.

"And if his offering is a goat, then he shall offer it before the Lord. He shall lay his hand on its head and kill it before the tabernacle of meeting; and the sons of Aaron shall sprinkle its blood all around on the altar. Then he shall offer from it his offering, as an offering made by fire to the Lord. The fat that covers the entrails and all the fat that is on the entrails, the two kidneys and the fat that is on them by the flanks, and the fatty lobe attached to the liver above the kidneys, he shall remove; and the priest shall burn them on the altar as food, an offering made by fire for a sweet aroma; all the fat is the Lord's.

"This shall be a perpetual statute throughout your generations in all your dwellings: you shall eat neither fat nor blood." (Lev. 3:1–17)

"This is the law of the sacrifice of peace offerings which he shall offer to the Lord:

"If he offers it for a thanksgiving, then he shall offer, with the sacrifice of thanksgiving, unleavened cakes mixed with oil, unleavened wafers anointed with oil, or cakes of finely blended flour mixed with oil. Besides the cakes, as his offering he shall offer leavened bread with the sacrifice of thanksgiving of his peace offering. And from it he shall offer one cake from each offering as a heave offering to the Lord. It shall belong to the priest who sprinkles the blood of the peace offering.

"The flesh of the sacrifice of his peace offering for thanksgiving shall be eaten the same day it is offered. He shall not leave any of it until the morning. But if the sacrifice of his offering is a vow or a voluntary offering, it shall be eaten the same day that he offers his sacrifice;

but on the next day the remainder of it also may be eaten; the remainder of the flesh of the sacrifice on the third day must be burned with fire. And if any of the flesh of the sacrifice of his peace offering is eaten at all on the third day, it shall not be accepted, nor shall it be imputed to him; whoever offers it shall be an abomination, and the person who eats of it shall bear guilt.

"The flesh that touches any unclean thing shall not be eaten. It shall be burned with fire. And as for the clean flesh, all who are clean may eat of it. But the person who eats the flesh of the sacrifice of the peace offering that belongs to the Lord, while he is unclean, that person shall be cut off from his people. Moreover the person who touches any unclean thing, such as human uncleanness, any unclean beast, or any abominable unclean thing, and who eats the flesh of the sacrifice of the peace offering that belongs to the Lord, that person shall be cut off from his people." (Lev. 7:11–21)

AS ALREADY pointed out, although the peace offering (called the fellowship offering in some translations) was third in the order set out in these early chapters of Leviticus, it was the last in the order of observance. In that place it is now to be considered. It was last in observance because peace comes to the soul as a result of complying with all that God has required.

Dr. J. A. Seiss points out that "the word *peace*, in the language of the Scriptures, has a shade of meaning not commonly attached to it in ordinary use. With most persons it signifies a cessation of hostilities, harmonious agreement, tranquility, the absence of disturbance. But in the Scripture it means more.

Its predominant import there is *prosperity, welfare, joy, happiness.* The original Hebrew word includes both of these meanings" (*The Gospel in Leviticus,* p. 64).

This, then, was a gathering together of the priests and the people with their God to rejoice in all the wonderful things that the Lord had done for them. It was a wonderful culmination of all that had transpired. As we consider it, may the same rejoicing be our experience.

Nature of the Offering—*Common to all. A cow or bull, a lamb, or a goat.* Each of these animals, which had to be without blemish, is characteristic of Christ in His perfect life upon earth.

The ox represents the Lord as the strong and patient One.

The lamb represents the Lord as the meek and gentle One.

The goat represents the Lord as the despised and rejected One.

While much of the book of Leviticus appears to be repetition, in fact it is not. The detail becomes part of the fascination of its study. Whereas in the other four offerings there was a variation of requirements according to the offerer—that is, according to possessions, according to property, according to position, and according to practice—in the peace offering there was no distinction at all. This offering was common to all.

What we note in the peace offering is the difference in . . .

(1) *The Victims.* While in some of the offerings

there were birds, these were not acceptable in the
peace offering. Two reasons would account for this.
In the first place, fat was an important essential because it was to be God's portion, but birds lacked
sufficient fat to meet the demand. Secondly, the peace
offering was the only one to be shared by three par-
ties. The birds would not be large enough for this
division.

(2) *The Sexes*. The animals could be male or female. In other instances, only the male was acceptable. Acceptability of both sexes here may speak of
a unity, a friendship factor related to the idea of
peace. Notice that a friendship which had not existed between God and man owing to sin had now
been established, because through the earlier offerings sin had been removed and now God and man
were brought together in a oneness. They were feasting together and fellowshiping together in a joyous
celebration.

(3) *The Treatment*. The burnt offering was a whole
burnt offering. All of it was for God. In the peace
offering, however, only the fat was offered to God.
God and priest and offerer all shared the blessings,
now complete.

While there were these differences, there were
also similarities. All offerings had to be without blemish. Where an animal was concerned, there was identification with its death and an application of the
blood, for without the shedding of blood there was
no remission. It is the blood which has opened a
new and living way to God, and by it we have salvation and peace.

The Offerer's Work—*Slay the offering*. "And he shall lay his hand on the head of his offering, and kill it at the door of the tabernacle of meeting" (Lev. 3:2).

The offerer had to lead the offering to the door of the tabernacle, lay his hand on the head of it as an act of identification, kill it, take out the fat that covered or was connected to the inner parts and give that to the priest to be burned. That was all. Man is required only to be obedient and give to God what is His due. That is, never give Him the leftovers or the part we can do without, but always the very best, the firstfruits. We shall see presently how important this is.

The Priest's Work—*Wave breast and shoulder*. The priest took the blood of the sacrifice and sprinkled it around the altar, after which he burned the fat upon the altar, ". . . the fat that covers the entrails and all the fat that is on the entrails, the two kidneys and the fat that is on them by the flanks, and the fatty lobe attached to the liver above the kidneys, he shall remove; and Aaron's sons shall burn it on the altar . . ." (Lev. 3:3–5). He then presented the breast and right shoulder to the Lord. "He who offers the sacrifice of his peace offering to the Lord shall bring his offering to the Lord from the sacrifice of his peace offering. His own hands shall bring the offerings made by fire to the Lord. The fat with the breast he shall bring, that the breast may be waved as a wave offering before the Lord. And the priest shall burn the fat on the altar . . ." (Lev. 7:29–31).

The breast denoted affection and the shoulder

represented strength. These should be yielded to the Lord. The priest, having presented these to the Lord, received them back from the Lord, as we receive back with interest all that we dedicate to Him and to His service.

God's Portion—*The fat on the entrails.* "Then he shall offer from it his offering, as an offering made by fire to the Lord. The fat that covers the entrails and all the fat that is on the entrails, the two kidneys and the fat that is on them by the flanks, and the fatty lobe attached to the liver above the kidneys, he shall remove; and the priest shall burn them on the altar as food, an offering made by fire for a sweet aroma; all the fat is the Lord's" (Lev. 3:14–16).

This fat was the fat of the inner organs, which is called suet, and not the fat that runs in the lean. It was considered the best part of the beast and was loved by the Easterner. It was required by God. Quoting from the *British Encyclopedia:* Fat is "an animal substitute of a more or less oily character, deposited in vessels, in tissues. It forms a considerable layer under the skin, is collected in large quantity around certain organs, as for instance, the kidneys, fills up furrows on the surface of the heart, surrounds joints, and exists in large quantities in the marrow of bones. It is an excellent packing material in the body, being light, soft, and elastic. Being a bad conductor of heat, it enables a person to retain the warmth he has generated, but its chief use is for the purpose of nutrition."

Fat is, therefore, that which protects the vital

life-giving, health-sustaining parts of the body, keeps the warmth, and feeds every part of the being. That is what the Lord requires—all that maintains spiritual life, keeps the warmth and love of our devotion, and feeds the soul with divine energy and a spiritual fervor.

Besides the fat of the inner organs, God had another requirement concerning the lambs. "Then he shall offer from the sacrifice of the peace offering, as an offering made by fire to the Lord, its fat and the whole fat tail which he shall remove close to the backbone . . ." (Lev. 3:9). There is a breed of sheep in the Middle East that grows a long and heavy tail, weighing as much as twenty pounds, most of which is fat. This part of the animal is considered sweet and valuable, and is greatly appreciated. Those bringing offerings loved this fat so much that if they could, they would keep part of the tail for themselves; hence the statements that the tail should be removed "close to the backbone," and "all the fat is the Lord's."

Fat burns very quickly and fiercely. This would suggest the readiness of the Lord to accept the best when it is offered to Him. When things are accepted by God they become sacred, and must no longer be treated as ordinary things. "Speak to the children of Israel, saying: 'You shall not eat any fat, of ox or sheep or goat. . . . For whoever eats the fat of the beast of which men offer an offering made by fire to the Lord, the person who eats it shall be cut off from his people'" (Lev. 7:23, 25).

The Priest's Portion—*Breast and shoulder*. This was the wave breast and the heave shoulder. There is a point of interest in the allocation of these portions. The breast is the symbol of affection. It went to the priesthood and was shared by the whole family, as the love and affection of the Lord is shared by all His children. The shoulder is the symbol of strength. This was for the particular priest who offered the particular sacrifice, a reminder that the strength of the Lord is given to those who serve.

The Offerer's Portion—*The remainder*. It was the only offering in which the offerer had a share. All that was left, after the Lord had received the fat and the priest had received the breast and right shoulder, was eaten by him and his friends in the court of the tabernacle. They were rejoicing in the finished work of their God.

The Typical Teaching—*Christ our Peace Offering*. Peace was declared when Christ was born. Said the angels: "Glory to God in the highest, and on earth *peace*, good will toward men" (Luke 2:14).

Peace was manifested in Christ's ministry: "Therefore, having been justified by faith, we have *peace* with God through our Lord Jesus Christ" (Rom 5:1).

Peace was secured through His death: ". . . and by Him to reconcile all things to Himself, by Him, whether things on earth or things in heaven, having made *peace* through the blood of His cross." (Col. 1:20).

Peace is ours through believing: "For He Himself is our *peace* [offering], who has made both one, and has broken down the middle wall of division between us" (Eph. 2:14).

The Symbolism—*Reconciliation*. Through all that Christ has accomplished upon the cross, through that one great sacrifice made once in the end of the age, He has perfected for us a complete reconciliation. We recognize and accept ". . . that God was in Christ reconciling the world to Himself, not imputing their trespasses to them, and has committed to us the word of reconciliation" (2 Cor. 5:19).

The peace offering ended in a joyous feasting together of priests and people with their God in the court of the tabernacle. This is intimated in Deuteronomy 12:5-7: "But you shall seek the place where the Lord your God chooses, out of all your tribes, to put his name for his habitation; and there you shall go. There you shall take your burnt offerings, your sacrifices, your tithes, the heave offerings of your hand, your vowed offerings, your freewill offerings, and the firstlings of your herds and flocks. and there you shall eat before the Lord your God, and you shall rejoice in all to which you have put your hand, you and your households, in which the Lord your God has blessed you." "You may not eat within your gates the tithe of your grain or your new wine or your oil, of the firstlings of your herd or your flock, of any of your offerings which you vow, of your freewill offerings, or of the heave offering of your hand. But you must eat them before the Lord your God in the place which the Lord your God chooses, you and your son and your daughter, your manservant and your maidservant, and the Levite who is within your gates; and you shall rejoice before the Lord your God in all to which you put your hands" (Deut. 12:17–18).

This feasting together in the fellowship of what has been accomplished by Christ, this *peace* which has been made sacred by the blood of His cross, this fellowship of believers, is to be celebrated in the sanctity of the church as it was then celebrated within the court of the tabernacle.

There is much service to be rendered for the Lord in the world. There is a testimony to be borne to unbelievers. There is our day-by-day Christian living, but there is also the spiritual feasting with the Lord and with the saints, feasting on His Word— which must be done in the place where He chooses to put His name. Did not Paul refer to this when he said ". . . not forsaking the assembling of ourselves together, as is the manner of some" (Heb. 10:25)?

Christ, having died, now lives, and we live in Him, feasting with Him, and sharing with others the peace of God that surpasses all understanding.

The Five Levitical Offerings
· Summary ·

The burnt offering was according to possession.
The grain offering was according to property.
The sin offering was according to position.
The trespass offering was according to practice.
The peace offering was common to all.

The burnt offering was Consecration of Self.
The grain offering was Consecration of Gifts.
The sin offering was Atonement.
The trespass offering was Restoration.
The peace offering was Reconciliation.

The burnt offering was
    Christ our Passover .... Eph. 5:2.
The grain offering was
    Christ the Kernel of Wheat .... John 12:24.
The sin offering was
    Christ our Sin Offering .... 2 Cor. 5:21.
The trespass offering was
    Christ our Trespass Offering .... Col. 2:13–14.
The peace offering was
    Christ our Peace Offering .... Eph. 2:14.

Part II

Your Reasonable Service

or

The Feasts of the Lord

· CHAPTER 1 ·

Introduction

THE book of Leviticus deals primarily with the worship of the people of God in the days prior to Christ's advent into this world. This worship was ordained by God and made known to man by divine revelation. While the details are practical and were given for man's observation, at the same time they were *typical*—they were a prefiguring of the claims of God and the worship of His people in the day of grace that would follow the advent of the Son of God. In this study both periods will be considered.

It has been pointed out in another book that the plan of Leviticus reveals God's great demand for holiness and His provision for it. This plan divides into two major sections, the first being the way to God through sacrifice. This has been considered in Part I in the five offerings, which have led man into a relationship with God wherein his sins have been dealt with and he is enjoying fellowship because of a peace that exists between God and man.

The second section is the walk with God through separation. Salvation is an act. Christianity is living Christ from day to day, walking with Him in a life of obedience. There are seven steps in this walk, and they are pictorialized in seven feasts known as the "Feasts of Jehovah." While the details of these feasts are to be found here and there, all seven are cata-logued in the twenty-third chapter of Leviticus.

They are called the feasts of the Lord because He appointed them. God not only established these feasts, He also designated the time of the year when they should be observed—March, May, and September, according to our calendar. They were set at seasons when it would be easy to travel, and also between the busy times of the year so far as an agricultural people were concerned. The Lord has no desire to make spiritual life a burden; He desires that it be a joyful experience. It is we who make it burdensome in always wanting to put selfish desires first.

The seven feasts were observed by all the males of Israel over a period of seven months. Although there were seven feasts, yet sometimes reference is made to three feasts. This is because the feasts were so spaced that three trips to Jerusalem were sufficient for the observance of all seven. "Three times in the year all your men shall appear before the Lord, the Lord God of Israel" (Exod. 34:23).

On their first journey to the capital city, which was in the first month of the year, three feasts were celebrated: the Feast of Passover on the evening of the fourteenth day, the Feast of Unleavened Bread from the fifteenth day and lasting for a whole week, and the Feast of Firstfruits on the sixteenth day. This group was known as "Passover," and became the first of the three journeys in which the people were involved.

A second journey was required seven weeks later for the observance of the Feast of Pentecost, which was on the sixteenth day of the third month. This feast was on its own. The remaining group of three feasts, known as "Tabernacles," required a third journey to the city. They were kept in the seventh month: the Feast of Trumpets on the first day of the month, the Day of Atonement on the tenth day, and the Feast of Tabernacles from the fifteenth until the twenty-second day.

The sequence of these feasts is very significant, revealing a divine plan and stamping the Bible with the seal of divine authority. The sequence not only reveals itself in the order of the feasts but it is manifested in the development of the Christian walk in the New Testament. The following study is set out in such a way as to reveal a threefold purpose:

(1) *The feast,* with all the ritual that belonged to the Old Testament days. This was set out by God, not merely for local observance but to be types, or pictures, setting forth various important truths. A type always anticipates.

(2) *An antitype,* or the New Testament fulfillment of the Old Testament symbol.

(3) *A spiritual application,* the same truths conveyed to the present day and applied to the progress of the Christian life.

Besides the seven annual feasts there were also the Sabbaths. These, too, were "feasts." There were the weekly Sabbaths and a number of special Sabbaths, which were all religious feasts. These were not seasons of feasting in relationship to food (in fact, one of them was a fast), but they were festive occasions during which the people forsook the everyday pursuits of life for a season of rejoicing in the Lord's goodness to them. They were called convocations. Today they would be referred to as conventions, when the people of the Lord meet together in fellowship and feast together in the exposition of His Word and the sharing of other spiritual blessings.

They were all seasons of rest. The repeated declaration was: "You shall do no customary work on it." In the case of the weekly Sabbath the Lord said: "Six days shall work be done, but the seventh day is a Sabbath of solemn rest, a holy convocation. You shall do no work on it; it is the Sabbath of the Lord in all your dwellings" (Lev. 23:3), meaning that it was a day free from work absolutely and entirely. "In all your dwellings" means in all parts of the land, in the home, hamlet, village, or town. What a repercussion would such a practice have upon our land if the Church of Jesus Christ were to observe the Lord's Day in this way! They did it under law—He still expects it under grace.

· CHAPTER 2 ·

The Sabbath

Speak to the children of Israel, and say to them: "The feasts of the Lord, which you shall proclaim to be holy convocations, these are my feasts. Six days shall work be done, but the seventh day is a Sabbath of solemn rest, a holy convocation. You shall do no work on it; it is the Sabbath of the Lord in all your dwellings." (Lev. 23:2–3)

BEFORE considering the annual conventions of Israel, known generally as the feasts of the Lord, time must be given to evaluate the weekly feast which is so often neglected, and yet it was a feast. It was the first on the list and its observance was much more frequent.

Lest anyone should read this with a biased mind, saying that this was Jewish or it was under the law, let it be understood that, while details sometimes change, principles never alter. The principle is that God demanded one day in seven, nature demands periodic rest, animals require rest other than nightly sleep, and even machinery functions better and wears longer when it has periodic rest. The fact that the Jews kept the seventh day and we the first is detail. Under law God demanded it; under grace He desires it. If we love certain people we seek to fulfill their desires and submit to their wishes because we know that, by so doing, we please them. Therefore, if God required certain things under law, we have reason to believe that He still is pleased by our fulfilling them under grace.

"The Sabbath was made for man, and not man for the Sabbath. Therefore the Son of Man is also Lord of the Sabbath" (Mark 2:27–28). The Sabbath day was not only given by God to man as a day of rest, but God expects man to give the same day back to Him in worship. How few there are who want to give this day to the Lord! Man is prepared to give God anything but time, and yet our times are in His hand. Man will give money, make a subscription to all sorts of things mentioned to him, give his approval to any kind of project the church may suggest—but not be willing to give his time. He considers Sunday to be his own, for his recreation, his pleasure, his family—as though it were the business world that has given him the day. Man has completely failed to recognize that it is the Lord's Day and that He gave it to man. Better yet, God set it apart for man, that in it he might rest from all his labors (which also means that he sees to it that others may also rest from their labors)—so that all of us might have time to relax, to think about spiritual things, to read spiritual matter, and to worship God. Let us examine it this way:

(1) *It was given for man's good.* The body needs periodic rest. Man cannot continually work seven days a week. Why are hospitals full? Why is it that there are no vacancies in mental institutions? Why is it that the public enemies of health are heart failure and ulcers? Overwork. Man wants to blame industry or the commercial world for pressure and over-

working. We know this is not true. There may be
pressure for five days—then man has a sixth day in
which he may relax and enjoy his pleasure, and a
seventh day to rest and worship God. If he did this
he would accomplish much more with less strain.
To question this procedure is foolish.

God rested on the seventh day from all His work.

Nature rests—fruit trees do not bear fruit every
year.

Ground needs to be rested—so the farmer leaves
his land fallow, or entirely changes his crop.

Machinery will operate better if it is allowed to
rest.

(2) *It was given for worship.* While the day was
given for rest, it was not given for indolence. While
the body rests, the mind is kept active with the things
of the Spirit. Man could worship any day; in fact he
should worship every day. However, collective worship is obviously best when we can blend our voices
in praise and listen to the exposition of the Word.
Therefore it is necessary to have a set time. Unless
there is a designated period there would be the risk
that public worship would soon cease to be.

If we realized what life would be like were this
day of worship taken away, most of us would value it
more than we do.

(3) *It was given by God.* If it be God's day then it
is a holy day, not a holiday; a day to be spent for
spiritual profit, not for selfish pleasure; a day to be
spent in worship, not a day at work. "Six days shall
work be done, but the seventh day is a Sabbath of
solemn rest, a holy convocation. You shall do no

work on it; it is the Sabbath of the Lord in all your dwellings" (Lev. 23:3).

In some of the feasts no customary work was to be done, which includes the activity of servants. In other feasts, including the Sabbath, "You shall do no work." This is all-embracive. No man should work, servant nor master, maid nor mistress. It was a day of rest, absolute and complete, not only in the home but everywhere, for the expression "in all your dwellings" infers "in all parts of the land and out of it," wherever the Jew might be living.

What a wonderful experience it would be if we could see *everything* at a standstill on a Sunday, no work being done, no one employed, all noise being silenced, people walking to church quietly and completely relaxed. That in itself, apart from the spiritual import, would be of immense value to mankind and to the nation, because we would be more relaxed through the week, pressures would yield, and we would be considerably healthier. The reaction would be seen in hospitals, in mental institutions, everywhere.

Some may say that this is impossible. There is nothing that is impossible. If a nation can change the whole of its policies in a time of war, if we can adjust to rations in war, if we can put satellites into space and also rendezvous in space, then this could be done if we had the desire. Some will assert that this was for the Jewish people and does not apply in the present dispensation. Then it must be understood that the Sabbath day was neither given *by*

Moses nor given *to* Moses. It existed long before the nation of Israel. The day is as old as man. God created man on the sixth day: "And on the seventh day God ended His work which He had done, and He rested on the seventh day from all His work which He had done. Then God blessed the seventh day and sanctified it." This means that it was set apart from the beginning of time. Later, this seventh day was incorporated into the law as the people were reminded to keep it holy.

The fourth commandment is the only one not repeated in the New Testament. Under the old order rest came at the end, but under the new order we begin with rest, because the Lord met all the demands of the law and we rest in an already finished work. Therefore, under grace, the first day of the week became the day set apart for rest and worship. Whether it be the seventh day for the Jew or the first day for the Christian, the principle remains exactly the same. One day in seven should be given to God. If we fail to make this day a day set apart to God and to the things that belong to the Spirit, then we have failed God and failed ourselves.

· CHAPTER 3 ·

The Feast of the Passover

Now the Lord spoke to Moses and Aaron in the land of Egypt, saying, "This month shall be your beginning of months; it shall be the first month of the year to you. Speak to all the congregation of Israel, saying: 'On the tenth day of this month every man shall take for himself a lamb, according to the house of his father, a lamb for a household. And if the household is too small for the lamb, let him and his neighbor next to his house take it according to the number of the persons; according to each man's need you shall make your count for the lamb. Your lamb shall be without blemish, a male of the first year. You may take it from the sheep or from the goats. Now you shall keep it until the fourteenth day of the same month. Then the whole assembly of the congregation of Israel shall kill it at twilight. And they shall take some of the blood and put it on the two doorposts and the lintel of the houses where they eat it. Then they shall eat the flesh on that night; roasted in fire, with unleavened bread and with bitter herbs they shall eat it. Do not eat it raw, nor boiled at all with water, but roasted in fire—its head with its legs and its entrails. You shall let none of it remain until morning, and what remains of it until morning you shall burn with fire. And thus you shall eat it: with a belt on your waist, your sandals on your feet, and your staff in your hand. So you shall eat it in haste. It is the Lord's Passover.

'For I will pass through the land of Egypt on that night, and will strike all the firstborn in the land of Egypt, both man and beast; and against all the gods of Egypt I will execute judgment: I am the Lord. Now the blood shall be a sign for you on the houses where you are. And when I see the blood, I will pass over you; and the plague shall not be on you to destroy you when I strike the land of Egypt.

'So this day shall be to you a memorial; and you shall keep it as a feast to the Lord throughout your generations. You shall keep it as a feast by an everlasting ordinance. Seven days you shall eat unleavened bread. On the first day you shall remove leaven from your houses. For whoever eats leavened bread from the first day until the seventh day, that person shall be cut off from Israel. On the first day there shall be a holy convocation, and on the seventh day there shall be a holy convocation for you. No manner of work shall be done on them; but that which everyone must eat—that only may be prepared by you.

'So you shall observe the Feast of Unleavened Bread, for on this same day I will have brought your armies out of the land of Egypt. Therefore you shall observe this day throughout your generations as an everlasting ordinance. In the first month, on the fourteenth day of the month at evening, you shall eat unleavened bread, until the twenty-first day of the month at evening. For seven days no leaven shall be found in your houses, since whoever eats what is leavened, that same person shall be cut off from the congregation of Israel, whether he is a stranger or a native of the land. You shall eat nothing leavened; in all your habitations you shall eat unleavened bread.'"

Then Moses called for all the elders of Israel and said to them, "Pick out and take lambs for yourselves according to your families, and kill the Passover lamb. And you shall take a bunch of hyssop, dip it in the blood that is in the basin, and strike the lintel and the two doorposts with the blood that is in the basin. And none of you shall go out of the door of his house until morning. For the Lord will pass through to strike the Egyptians; and when He sees the blood on the lintel and on the two doorposts, the Lord will pass over the door and not allow the destroyer to come into your houses to strike you. And you shall observe this thing as an ordinance for you and your sons forever. It will come to pass when you come to the land which the Lord will give you, just as He promised, that you shall keep this service. And it shall be, when your children say to you, 'What do you mean by this service?' that you shall say, 'It is the Passover sacrifice of the Lord, who passed over the houses of the children of Israel in Egypt when He struck the Egyptians and delivered our households.'" So the people bowed their heads and worshiped. Then the children of Israel went away and did so; just as the Lord had commanded Moses and Aaron, so they did.

And it came to pass at midnight that the Lord struck all the firstborn in the land of Egypt, from the firstborn of Pharaoh who sat on his throne to the firstborn of the captive who was in the dungeon, and all the firstborn of livestock. So Pharaoh rose in the night, he, all his servants, and all the Egyptians; and there was a great cry in Egypt, for there was not a house where there was not one dead. (Exod. 12:1–30)

THIS ACCOUNT is well known, since it has been retold so many times; therefore, the salient points of the story will suffice. Israel had been in Egypt a long time (in fact, 430 years—see Exod. 12:40), and many changes had taken place. Their

entrance into the land had everything in their favor, with all the blessings of Pharaoh resting upon
them. Their exit was very different; indeed, nothing
was in their favor. Instead of enjoying the freedom
of the land, they had become slaves; instead of having the best, they were enduring the worst the task-
masters could lay on them. Instead of the blessings
of Pharaoh, it was the cursings of another Pharaoh
"who did not know Joseph," a ruler who was fearful
of the power that might be manifested by an alien
people within his domain. And yet, while all this
was true, their sufferings, like most of ours, were self-
imposed—brought upon them by their own self-will
and rebellion. The first Pharaoh had been favorable
to them because they were in favor with God. The
last Pharaoh was opposing them because they, as a
people, were opposing God and, therefore, God had
turned His back on them.

Now God had heard their cry, and was coming
down to deliver them. Not only was He about to
bring deliverance to His own people, but He was
also in the process of punishing the nation that had
found delight in being cruel to the children of Israel. Already God had inflicted nine plagues upon
the Egyptians, every one of them proving how helpless were the gods of Egypt, for the Israelites had
been immune to every plague. Egypt's gods had not
checked one of the plagues nor alleviated the sufferings of their worshipers. The tenth and final plague
was about to be administered. It was the death of
the firstborn of every Egyptian family, including the
royal household. Not only was this to be a great

tragedy in the communal life of all Egypt, but it was to be the greatest blow to their religious system, for the Egyptians never accepted death. They abominated the thought of it, and as a result they worshiped everything that symbolized life. They believed in the transmigration of spirits and so made preparation for the journey of one's spirit into its next realm.

This event was going to be so sudden and so disastrous that the Lord began to prepare His people for their emancipation before the blow fell upon the nation, and to enable His people to make a complete exodus before Pharaoh could again change his mind. The plan was made by God. The instructions were clear and simple. The scheme might not appear logical in the thinking of man, but all that was required was obedience.

The event was going to be so stupendous in the lives of these oppressed people and in the future of their nation that God changed the calendar. It happened in the fourth month of the year, but God said: "This month shall be your beginning of months; it shall be the first month of the year to you" (Exod. 12:2). The rest of the story will be considered under the title . . .

The Feast. Much of it became an annual event. On the tenth day of the month a lamb was to be taken for each family. It was to be kept for four days to prove it was without blemish. On the fourteenth day it was slain and the blood was sprinkled upon the two door posts and the upper lintel, for protection from the angel of death came only by *applied* blood. Blood in a bowl in the house, or blood merely shed, was not sufficient. It had to be applied where it could be seen, for, said the Lord: "And when I see the blood, I will pass over you; and the plague shall not be on you to destroy you when I strike the land of Egypt" (Exod. 12:13). Salvation is not our project—it is His provision.

Inside the house, protected by that blood, the people prepared to feast upon the lamb that had been slain. The feast also included bitter herbs and unleavened bread. Instead of taking the meal leisurely, they were required to have their belts fastened as for a journey, their sandals on their feet, their staves in their hands, ready to make a speedy exit, for the day of their emancipation had come. God was meting out vengeance on their enemies and on Pharaoh who had so stubbornly refused to let them go. He was now prepared to drive them out. When God's time had fully come, bondage was suddenly changed into glorious liberty. This was the beginning of a new life. Therefore they had to leave the old conditions before they became entangled again.

This feast, as considered so far, was a historical event. It took place once only. However, certain events were established to be observed annually as memorials, lest the people forget the goodness of God. Thus we read: "These are the feasts of the Lord, holy convocations which you shall proclaim at their appointed times. On the fourteenth day of the first month at twilight is the Lord's Passover" (Lev. 23:4–5).

Antitype. This feast is not only observed as a

commemorative rite to remind Israel of a past deliverance, but it is also an occasion to remind these people of a greater deliverance yet to come.

When Jesus began His public ministry ". . . John saw Jesus coming toward him, and said, 'Behold! the Lamb of God who takes away the sin of the world!'" (John 1:29). For years the Jewish nation had offered a lamb from the first Passover night until the days of the New Testament. That lamb had reminded them of God's past deliverance. Now John was pointing out to these same people that before them stood *the* Lamb of God, the One whom they had long anticipated. God was now turning their shadows into substance, their anticipations into realization, the type into antitype. Here was the Emancipator, the One who was to pardon all sin.

The Passover lamb of the commemorative rite had to be kept four days before it was slain to establish proof that it was without blemish. *The* Lamb of God, now introduced to the nation, engaged in three and a half years of public ministry where all could behold Him, check His life and ministry, and establish the fact that He was without sin, the perfect Son of God. This evidence was given just before He died:

Judas said: "I have sinned by betraying innocent blood" (Matt. 27:4).

Pilate said: "I am innocent of the blood of this just person" (Matt. 27:24).

Pilate's wife said: "Have nothing to do with that just man" (Matt. 27:19).

Pilate said: "I find no fault in him at all" (John 18:38).

The malefactor said: ". . . but this man has done nothing wrong" (Luke 23:41).

The centurion said: "Truly this man was the Son of God!" (Mark 15:39).

All these testimonies concerning the sinless One came from His enemies and from the general public. Peter, Stephen and Paul bore the same record, and so did His Father.

Without blemish though He was, yet He was taken by wicked hands and crucified. Paul, referring back to this, said: "For indeed Christ, our passover, was sacrificed for us" (1 Cor. 5:7). ". . . and without shedding of blood there is no remission" (Heb. 9:22).

Spiritual Application—*Salvation.* We must bear in mind that by nature we are sinners and that we are in the Egypt of this world which is ruled over by Satan. Under his regime men become slaves and are doomed to eternal destruction.

In this helpless condition that was the lot of man, God sent His Son to become the Lamb of God. As the Lamb He died at Calvary, that through the shedding of His blood salvation might come to all men. The event itself is history. It may be called religion, doctrine, theology, or anything else, but it was God's plan and there is no alternative. One of the great essentials in the Passover story was that man had to take the blood of the lamb and apply it to his own house, with the promise: "And when I see the blood, I will pass over you." This essential remains true today. It is not sufficient to be born in a country called "Christian" because it accepts certain facts of history, or because one finds himself in a Christian community where he has been taught to go to church and to accept in principle the things preached there. There must be a personal acceptance of the blood of Jesus Christ applied to the heart and life, a personal understanding that Christ died for my sin, that His blood accepted can wash away my sin, and that in so doing the condemnation of death which is my due can be removed.

This act, whereby we accept in simple faith and obedience the efficacy of the blood of Christ shed upon the cross as the cleansing for our sin, is called . . .

Salvation. Man passes from death unto life, from bondage into liberty, from darkness into light. He is leaving an old life for a new one. He is entering into an entirely new experience.

Having walked *to* God through sacrifice, he now begins his walk *with* God through separation. In other words, salvation is not an end, it is a beginning. Thus the Lord says: "This month shall be your beginning of months."

This new life should be one of great excitement as the believer grows from a babe in Christ into the mature life of the disciple. Spiritual life must know the same growth, development of character, and maturity of experience that takes place in the natural life—but with one tremendous difference. In the physical body a certain point of development is reached and then, suddenly, we are aware that we have passed our prime. Now come reminders of decline: mental alertness may give way, memory may fail, energy weakens, and we are reminded that whatever has been accomplished in the way of success, whatever has been acquired in material possessions, however great the host of friends we have made, one day we shall lose everything. The finality of the physical realm is death, and as surely as we brought nothing into the world, so surely we will take nothing out of it. The soul, which knows no death, leaves this present world to inhabit another realm.

The thrill and excitement of our new life, which is inherited at salvation, is one of continuous development and knows no end. Our physical body declines, but our spirit matures. Earthly success terminates, but spiritual success has rewards awaiting in the life to come. While material possessions are left behind, spiritual possessions are treasures laid up in heaven where neither moth nor rust corrupt and where thieves do not break through nor steal. We may bid adieu to our friends on earth, but the Christian is reunited with them in heaven. We anticipate the fellowship in heaven.

Our journey is toward a promised inheritance and an eternal rest. Having begun this walk on earth, let us take the next step.

· Chapter 4 ·

The Feast of Unleavened Bread

"Seven days you shall eat unleavened bread. On the first day you shall remove leaven from your houses. For whoever eats leavened bread from the first day until the seventh day, that person shall be cut off from Israel. On the first day there shall be a holy convocation, and on the seventh day there shall be a holy convocation for you. No manner of work shall be done on them; but that which everyone must eat—that only may be prepared by you.

"So you shall observe the Feast of Unleavened Bread, for on this same day I will have brought your armies out of the land of Egypt. Therefore you shall observe this day throughout your generations as an everlasting ordinance. In the first month, on the fourteenth day of the month at evening, you shall eat unleavened bread, until the twenty-first day of the month at evening. For seven days no leaven shall be found in your houses, since whoever eats what is leavened, that same person shall be cut off from the congregation of Israel, whether he is a stranger or a native of the land. You shall eat nothing leavened; in all your habitations you shall eat unleavened bread." (Exod. 12:15–20)

And Moses said to the people: "Remember this day in which you went out of Egypt, out of the house of bondage; for by strength of hand the Lord brought you out of this place. No leavened bread shall be eaten. On this day you are going out, in the month Abib. And it shall be, when the Lord brings you into the land of the Canaanites and the Hittites and the Amorites and Hivites and Jebusites, which He swore to your fathers to give you, a land flowing with milk and honey, that you shall keep this service in this month. Seven days you shall eat unleavened bread, and on the seventh day there shall be a feast to the Lord. Unleavened bread shall be eaten seven days. And no leavened bread shall be seen among you, nor shall leaven be seen among you in all your quarters. And you shall tell your son in that day, saying, 'This is done because of what the Lord did for me when I came up from Egypt.' It shall be as a sign to you on your hand and as a memorial between your eyes, that the Lord's law may be in your mouth; for with a strong hand the Lord has brought you out of Egypt. You shall therefore keep this ordinance in its season from year to year." (Exod. 13:3–10)

THE FEAST of Unleavened Bread was included in the Passover feast, which accounts for the overlap of dates. Both feasts began on the fourteenth day of the first month. The one was a single-day celebration, the other was observed for seven days. The number seven being symbolic of completeness means that whatever was inferred by the feast involved the complete life. There are many scattered verses which, when brought together, make a complete picture.

The Feast. "In the first month, on the fourteenth day of the month at evening, you shall eat unleavened bread, until the twenty-first day of the month at evening. For seven days no leaven shall be found in your houses, since whoever eats what is leavened, that same person shall be cut off from the congregation of Israel, whether he is a stranger or a native of the land. You shall eat nothing leavened; in all your habitations you shall eat unleavened bread" (Exod. 12:18–20).

Although the Feast of Unleavened Bread as such began on the fifteenth day—"on the fifteenth day of the same month is the Feast of Unleavened Bread to the Lord . . ." (Lev. 23:6)—yet leavened bread was not to be eaten at the Passover, which was on the fourteenth day. Therefore, the preceding day was called "the Day of Preparation." We read: "On the next day, which followed the Day of Preparation . . ." (Matt. 27:62). And: "Now it was the Preparation Day of the Passover . . ." (John 19:14).

This day involved a great time of spring-cleaning. No leaven was allowed within their dwellings. It meant more than simply not eating leaven. It was a matter of complete separation. This, therefore, meant a great deal of activity for the woman in each house. Everything in the house had to be cleansed thoroughly. The ceilings and walls were washed, floors and cupboards were scrubbed, corners were scoured, and every piece of furniture cleaned. All the cooking utensils were boiled in water and put away, while special utensils and ovens were brought into use— things that had never been contaminated by leaven in the course of the year. So thoroughly was this work done that the woman had a pointed tool with which she would scrape through every crack or joint, impression or corner, any spot where, during the year, a crumb of bread containing leaven might have settled. The law was that no leaven should remain anywhere within their dwellings. Each household carried out the law strictly to the letter.

When the cleansing was complete, a member of the household would take pieces of leavened bread and tuck each piece in a hiding place, somewhere around the house—a piece under a cushion, or on a ledge, or behind a vessel. At the day's close, when the man of the house had returned from the fields and had partaken of his evening meal—and after the sun had set—there would take place in each home a light-hearted ceremony known as the "search for leaven." Taking a lighted candle, a feather brush, and a wooden spoon, the father would search for the pieces of leavened bread which had previously been hidden. The children, who had earlier taken note of where the bread had been placed, would help their father by telling him that he was getting hot and hotter, or cold and colder, as he advanced toward or retreated from the various pieces (a game with which many of us are acquainted). As he gathered each piece he would recite a prayer: "Blessed art Thou, O Lord our God, King of the Universe, who hast sanctified us with Thy commandments and commanded us to remove the leaven."

He then wrapped the pieces in a cloth and said: "All kinds of leaven that are in my possession which I have not observed nor removed, shall be null and counted as the dust of the earth." Next morning, with similar prayers, he burned the pieces.

Having done all that was within their power to remove the leaven, they trusted God to annul or destroy anything they had accidentally missed. They were now ready for the observance of the feast.

Only unleavened bread could be eaten. This was made of white flour, ground in special mills, and its making was superintended by a wise man of the law. The dough was made of flour and water only. No yeast or salt must be added. It was then rolled into flat cakes, pierced and pricked all over, and baked in a specially prepared oven, very hot. On this bread the children of Israel lived for eight days.

It is recorded in the book of Exodus how all of these commands and observances were passed down from generation to generation: "And you shall tell your son in that day, saying, 'This is done because of what the Lord did for me when I came up from Egypt'" (Exod. 13:8).

The whole purpose of this feast was to teach the people that they were to be disassociated from their old life. They were to keep themselves from the carnalities of the world around them. They were a holy people separated to the Lord their God. Yeast was a type of that other world.

Lest they should forget this requirement of God, He established this feast to be an annual event and hence a continuing reminder.

Some people think that the children of Israel routinely ate unleavened bread during their years of sojourn in Egypt. This is incorrect. Yeast belonged to Egypt and the world. It was a type of sin and belonged to the old life. The unleavened bread that they were instructed to eat the night of the Passover (Exod. 12:8) belonged to the new life. One evidence that they did not regularly eat this bread in Egypt is found in the account of their departure from the land. Through the urgency of the Egyptians, the people were driven out before they could resume baking their usual leavened bread. "So the people took their dough before it was leavened, having their kneading bowls bound up in their clothes on their shoulders. . . . Then the children of Israel journeyed from Rameses to Succoth" (Exod. 12:34, 37).

It has been pointed out that unleavened bread belonged to the new life. The unleavened bread that they carried out of Egypt they ate at Succoth in the wilderness. "Then the children of Israel journeyed from Rameses to Succoth, about six hundred thousand men on foot, besides children. A mixed multitude went up with them also, and flocks and herds—a great deal of livestock. And they baked unleavened cakes of the dough which they had brought out of Egypt; for it was not leavened, because they were driven out of Egypt and could not wait, nor had they prepared provisions for themselves" (Exod. 12:37–39).

Antitype. As the Jew in the Old Testament was very conscientious about being rid of all leaven for a particular period, so the same truth is propounded in the New Testament concerning this Church age and must become the responsibility of every believer in Christ.

Paul, writing to the saints in the Corinthian church, left us without any shadow of a doubt: "Therefore purge out the old leaven, that you may be a new lump, since you truly are unleavened. For indeed Christ, our Passover, was sacrificed for us.

Therefore let us keep the feast, not with old leaven, nor with the leaven of malice and wickedness, but with the unleavened bread of sincerity and truth" (1 Cor. 5:7–8).

Leaven promotes fermentation and corruption. A little of it will bring a whole batch of dough into an upheaval. It quickly permeates the whole. Therefore it is used in Scripture as a type of sin. Sin had crept into the Corinthian church. Paul required that this leaven should be removed from that church because God demanded holiness.

When Paul wrote to them he was not writing to unsaved sinners but to the saints who had been responsible for allowing this intrusion. Sin is like leaven. A little of it goes a long way, and its influence is considerable.

God's concern for Israel was contamination, the influence that the nations around them could have on a separated nation. It was for the same reason that the Lord would not allow His people to intermingle through marriage. "Therefore, 'Come out from among them, and be separate,' says the Lord. 'Do not touch what is unclean, and I will receive you. I will be a Father to you, and you shall be My sons and daughters,' says the Lord Almighty" (2 Cor. 6:17–18).

Spiritual Application—*Separation*. As surely as the Feast of Unleavened Bread immediately followed the Passover and was in fact a part of it, so the life of sanctification—the life that is one of separation from the world, the flesh, and the devil—begins with our salvation and should continue for the remainder of life's journey on earth, inasmuch as the period of seven days is the symbol of the complete life. This life ought not to be continually reached after and never attained. It should be an experience that is enjoyed at all times. When he is saved, the believer dies to self that he may live for Christ; hence he has a new life—a life full of new experiences—a life that is lived by God's enabling. It is a life totally different from the one that belonged to the world, for it is the outliving of the Spirit's indwelling.

Many people have the idea that during that week the nation refrained merely from the eating of leavened bread; but let the fact be underscored that no leaven was to be found *anywhere* in their dwellings— it was not to be within the camp.

May we be permitted to use a personal illustration? The author, in one of his earlier pastorates, went to his church each morning for a period of time in order to make a church alteration. He went in by a back door and stayed the whole morning. The church was situated on a main road facing a row of shops. A member of the church, a teenage girl who was not working at the time, discovered the situation. About an hour later than his arrival each morning, she wandered into the church by the same back door and just stood around talking. This she did to pass her time away, having nothing else to do. This happened for three mornings. On the fourth day, when she arrived he took her to the front of the church and, opening the front doors, pointed out that on the other side of the street was a shoe repairer sitting near his window, and a butcher and a grocer both serving merchandise near open windows. The probability was that these people had witnessed the arrival of the minister and, later, the arrival of the girl. This would surely suggest that a man and a girl were together in a closed church. Might not the situation put unseemly thoughts and ideas into the minds of these people? Was it not possible that, although the girl came in innocently to have a chat, rumors might be circulated that could be damaging to the church? The girl was told to go home and never to come into the church again when the pastor was there alone. This decision was made in order to "abstain from all *appearance* of evil" (1 Thess. 5:22).

It is not enough that we do not commit sin, but we must walk so circumspectly that we do not give the world a single opportunity to accuse us. Are we living this new life, or are we so mixed up with the world and worldly ambitions—and participating in its pleasures, fashions and customs—that it becomes difficult to distinguish the one from the other?

Must we not also confess that a great deal of the world and its carnalities have crept into the church? In our compromise to win the world, we have lost the world and our own testimony.

God lays claim to our regenerated life. Have we made this second step? Is our all upon the altar? Is He our satisfying portion? Are we living the life that is dead to self and alive to Christ? If so, we are ready for the next step in this "walk with God through separation."

· Chapter 5 ·

The Feast of Firstfruits

And the Lord spoke to Moses, saying, "Speak to the children of Israel, and say to them: 'When you come into the land which I give to you, and reap its harvest, then you shall bring a sheaf of the firstfruits of your harvest to the priest. He shall wave the sheaf before the Lord, to be accepted on your behalf; on the day after the Sabbath the priest shall wave it. And you shall offer on that day, when you wave the sheaf, a male lamb of the first year, without blemish, as a burnt offering to the Lord. Its grain offering shall be two-tenths of an ephah of fine flour mixed with oil, an offering made by fire to the Lord, for a sweet aroma; and its drink offering shall be of wine, one-fourth of a hin. You shall eat neither bread nor parched grain nor fresh grain until the same day that you have brought an offering to your God; it shall be a statute forever throughout your generations in all your dwellings.'" (Lev. 23:9–14)

THIS FEAST was closely associated with the two that have gone before, since all had to do with the Passover itself and were held consecutively on the fourteenth, fifteenth, and sixteenth days of the first month. Although the Passover was established on the night the children of Israel left Egypt, it was not observed as a commemorative feast during the forty years they were wandering in the wilderness. This was not because they had no lambs, for they did; nor was it because the people were being sustained primarily by the manna which God provided from day to day. But for some reason, after keeping the Passover on the night of their deliverance, they never observed it again until they entered the Promised Land. At that time "the children of Israel camped in Gilgal, and kept the Passover on the fourteenth day of the month at twilight on the plains of Jericho" (Joshua 5:10).

Likewise, this Feast of Firstfruits was not observed until the nation had entered the Promised Land. Until this time they had eaten only manna and whatever their flocks and herds provided. In the desert they were a roaming people who had no fields to sow nor harvests to reap. But God told Moses: "Speak to the children of Israel, and say unto them: 'When you come into the land which I give to you, and reap its harvest, then you shall bring a sheaf of the firstfruits of your harvest to the priest'" (Lev. 23:10). This would be barley, because that was the first grain to ripen. After the barley would come the harvesting of the fruit, the olives, the vintage, and finally the wheat.

The Feast. The account of the feast, so far as the ceremony in the house of God was concerned, is recorded in Leviticus 23. However, we need to turn to the pages of history and to the customs of these people in order to gain information as to the preliminaries to the feast.

During most of the Roman period, the internal government of Judea was controlled by the Sanhedrin, a group of elders presided over by the high priest. At the time of seed sowing, members of the Sanhedrin would have marked off certain barley fields by going out to three of the fields within the vicinity of the city of Jerusalem and laying in each field a hoop, thereby ringing off that seed. These were left there until the seed germinated, sprang up, and matured. By the time the harvest season arrived, the hoops would be hidden under the ripened grain.

It must be borne in mind that this feast was kept on the sixteenth day, and that the day began at six o'clock in the evening (hence the repeated statement in Genesis 1: "And the evening and the morning were a day."). Toward the close of the fifteenth day, just before the going down of the sun, three men, each carrying a sickle and a basket, walked out through the city gate. Separating, each one would move toward one of the three buried hoops and stand there. These men were accompanied by representatives of the people, both secular and religious—in other words, elders and priests—who would wait outside the city gate. Quietly they would watch the sun set, denoting the end of that day. As it slipped over the horizon the three men would address the priest with the following questions:

"Has the sun gone down?"

"On this fifteenth day?"

"Into this basket?" (Each man would hold the basket above his head.)

"With this sickle?" (Holding it high for all to see.)

"Shall I reap?"

To each question the priest would answer in the affirmative. With the last "yes," the three men would simultaneously thrust their sickles into the barley within the hoops, and the sheaves would be placed in the baskets. Then these men, with the priests and elders, would march processionally up to the temple with much rejoicing, where the bundles would be put together into one great sheaf and handed to the priest. He, in turn, took the sheaf and waved it before the Lord as a wave offering. This was in accordance with the command: "When you come into the land which I give to you, and reap its harvest, then you shall bring a sheaf of the firstfruits of your harvest to the priest. He shall wave the sheaf before the Lord, to be accepted on your behalf; on the day after the Sabbath the priest shall wave it" (Lev. 23: 10–11). This wave sheaf was accompanied by burnt offerings and grain offerings.

Until the wave sheaf was offered ". . . you shall eat neither bread nor parched grain nor fresh grain until the same day that you have brought an offering to your God" (Lev. 23:14). This meant that no man was permitted to partake of any part of the new season's harvest until the firstfruits had been presented.

The waving of the sheaf from one side to the other before the Lord indicated that it represented the whole harvest yet in the field, from one end of the land to the other. By this action, men gave thanks to God for the harvest while it still stood in the fields. God has always claimed the firstfruits of everything. He still does.

Antitype. What a wonderful picture of our Lord Jesus Christ who, having become the Paschal Lamb shedding His blood upon the cross, is afterwards seen in the fullness of His resurrection power. Said Paul: "But now Christ is risen from the dead, and has become the firstfruits of those who have fallen asleep" (1 Cor. 15:20). He was the kernel of grain that fell into the ground and died, that it might spring up again and produce much fruit. The Feast of Firstfruits was the third day following Passover. Christ rose as the firstfruits of resurrection on the third day after His death.

As the sheaf was a memorial or a representation of the whole harvest in the field, so Christ, when He arose from the dead, said to Mary: "Do not cling to Me, for I have not yet ascended to My Father; but go to My brethren, and say to them, 'I am ascending to My Father and your Father, and to My God and your God'" (John 20:17).

The Lord is now in the presence of His Father as the representative of the whole Church of Jesus Christ still in the field. He has promised: ". . . because I live, you shall live also." He will remain the firstfruits and our representative until the day of His coming again, when the whole harvest of the Church, including those who are in the graves and we who are alive and remain, shall be gathered in for the great "Harvest Home."

When the sheaves were cut from the fields and carried to the city, small vacant spots were left behind. When the Lord rose from the dead, He left behind a small vacant spot which still remains as a reminder of His resurrection—an empty tomb.

During the time the grain was growing in the

field, it enjoyed the warmth of the sun and withstood the winds, storms, and all the elements of adverse weather. Thus it is with the child of God. So long as he is in this world he will know something of the adverse winds that toss him about at times and the drought that wilts his faith at other times; but he can also bask in the warmth of God's love and find the reinvigoration that comes in the rays of His mercy and in the dew of His grace. It takes all of these experiences, the adverse and the acceptable, to develop our fruitfulness so that we will not be ashamed at His coming. Remember that the Sheaf of Firstfruits, who has gone before, knew all these same experiences.

Spiritual Application—*Consecration*. This is the third step in the Christian walk—the first, salvation; the second, separation; the third, consecration. Separation, as seen in the unleavened bread, far-reaching as it was, proved to be insufficient by itself. At least God thought so, for He required more. Likewise, separation in the Christian life is not the end of God's requirements—He asks for consecration.

A question which might come immediately to mind would be: What is the difference? In the first, it is separation *from*; in the second, separation *to*. If one only separates from the world, or from anything else, and seeks to stand alone, he could very readily become an isolationist. This is not practicable because there is too much involved in life. The Lord illustrated this point with a parable told in Luke 11:17–26. The Lord was casting out a demon. He was separating a man from the power of an old life, and there were those who questioned His authority. In His reply to His critics He said that a kingdom divided against itself would be ruined, and a house divided against itself would fall. Division is a weakening thing in itself, and the reason is: "When an unclean spirit goes out of a man, he goes through dry places, seeking rest; and finding none, he says, 'I will return to my house from which I came.' And when he comes, he finds it swept and put in order. Then he goes and takes with him seven other spirits more wicked than himself, and they enter and dwell there; and the last state of that man is worse than the first." If a person leaves one thing he must be attached to something else. He cannot be independent. To think that salvation means only separation from the world is a tragedy because, although we may not be of the world, we are in it and we are surrounded. In fact, we are pressured by its temptations, its pleasures, its moral issues in business as well as in social and political life. It is impossible for any individual to resist this massive force. Therefore, as soon as we separate *from* the old life we must separate ourselves *unto* the Lord Jesus Christ, the only source of power. This is what is understood by consecration.

It may help us to appreciate this thought by seeing it in operation in everyday life.

A piece of land is consecrated when it is separated *to* burial—a cemetery.

A building is consecrated when it is separated *to* the worship of God—a church.

A man is consecrated when he is separated *to* the

work of the ministry—a minister.

We consecrate ourselves when we separate our lives and will *to* the purposes of God.

It must be emphasized that this feast was held on the sixteenth day, and is the third step of the Passover, or salvation. The believer, therefore, ought to give the firstfruits of his life, the best part of it, the early years if converted early—yes, himself—and yield them without reserve to the Lord, remembering that "you are not your own. For you were bought at a price; therefore glorify God in your body and in your spirit, which are God's" (1 Cor. 6:19–20).

As no person was allowed to move a sickle in the field until the firstfruits were presented, so we take nothing to ourselves until we have presented our all to Him.

> My spirit, soul, and body,
> Jesus, I give to Thee,
> A consecrated off'ring,
> Thine evermore to be.
> My all is on the altar,
> Lord, I am all Thine own;
> Oh, may my faith ne'er falter,
> Lord, keep me Thine alone.

When we have yielded our all, then He will give us back our lives—endued, equipped, blessed.

> Take my life, and let it be
> Consecrated, Lord, to Thee.

· Chapter 6 ·

The Feast of Pentecost

"And you shall count for yourselves from the day after the Sabbath, from the day that you brought the sheaf of the wave offering: seven Sabbaths shall be completed. Count fifty days to the day after the seventh Sabbath; then you shall offer a new grain offering to the Lord. You shall bring from your habitations two wave loaves of two-tenths of an ephah. They shall be of fine flour; they shall be baked with leaven. They are the firstfruits to the Lord. And you shall offer with the bread seven lambs of the first year, without blemish, one young bull, and two rams. They shall be as a burnt offering to the Lord, with their grain offering and their drink offerings, an offering made by fire for a sweet aroma to the Lord. Then you shall sacrifice one kid of the goats as a sin offering, and two male lambs of the first year as a sacrifice of peace offering. The priest shall wave them with the bread of the firstfruits as a wave offering before the Lord, with the two lambs. They shall be holy to the Lord for the priest. And you shall proclaim on the same day that it is a holy convocation to you. You shall do no customary work on it. It shall be a statute forever in all your dwellings throughout your generations.

"When you reap the harvest of your land, you shall not wholly reap the corners of your field when you reap, nor shall you gather any gleaning from your harvest. You shall leave them for the poor and for the stranger: I am the Lord your God." (Lev. 23:15–22)

Now when the Day of Pentecost had fully come, they were all with one accord in one place. And suddenly there came a sound from heaven, as of a rushing mighty wind, and it filled the whole house where they were sitting. Then there appeared to them divided tongues, as of fire, and one sat upon each of them. And they were all filled with the Holy Spirit and began to speak with other tongues, as the Spirit gave them utterance.

Now there were dwelling in Jerusalem Jews, devout men, from every nation under heaven. And when this sound occurred, the multitude came together, and were confused, because everyone heard them speak in his own language. Then they were all amazed and marveled, saying to one another, "Look, are not all these who speak Galileans? And how is it that we hear, each in our own language in which we were born? Parthians and Medes and Elamites, those dwelling in Mesopotamia, Judea and Cappadocia, Pontus and Asia, Phrygia and Pamphylia, Egypt and the parts of Libya adjoining Cyrene, visitors from Rome, both Jews and proselytes, Cretans and Arabs—we hear them speaking in our own tongues the wonderful works of God." So they were all amazed and perplexed, saying to one another, "Whatever could this mean?"

Others mocking said, "They are full of new wine."

But Peter, standing up with the eleven, raised his voice and said to them, "Men of Judea and all who dwell in Jerusalem, let this be known to you, and heed my words. For these are not drunk, as you suppose, since it is only the third hour of the day. But this is what was spoken by the prophet Joel:

'And it shall come to pass in the last days, says God, that I will pour out of My Spirit on all flesh; your sons and your daughters shall prophesy, your young men shall see visions, your old men shall dream dreams. And on My menservants and on My maidservants I will pour out My Spirit in those days; and they shall prophesy. I will show wonders in heaven above and signs in the earth beneath: blood and fire and vapor of smoke. The sun shall be turned into darkness, and the moon into blood, before the coming of the great and notable day of the Lord. And it shall come to pass that whoever calls on the name of the Lord shall be saved.' . . ."

Now when they heard this, they were cut to the heart, and said to Peter and the rest of the apostles, "Men and brethren, what shall we do?"

Then Peter said to them, "Repent, and let every one of you be baptized in the name of Jesus Christ for the remission of sins; and you shall receive the gift of the Holy Spirit. For the promise is to you and to your children, and to all who are afar off, as many as the Lord our God will call."

And with many other words he testified and exhorted them, saying, "Be saved from this perverse generation." Then those who gladly received his word were baptized; and that day about three thousand souls were added to them. (Acts 2:1–21, 37–41)

FOLLOWING the Feast of Firstfruits there were no other feasts for seven weeks. The children of Israel having presented their firstfruits to God, and He having received them, the harvesting began. This was a busy season for the people. It took the whole seven weeks for the ingathering. It has already been mentioned that it began with the barley harvest, which ripened in April. By the time the barley was in, the fruit was ready, after which the olives were gathered. Then the vineyards became hives of activity with the vintage, and the season concluded with the ingathering of the wheat.

As there was a feast to acknowledge the firstfruits, so there was one to commemorate Harvest Home. In the Old Testament it is spoken of as the Feast of Weeks (Exod. 34:22; Deut. 16:10,16; 2 Chron. 8:13). In the New Testament it is called Pentecost, because *pente* in Greek is "fifty," and this took place fifty days after the presentation of the wave sheaf.

Owing to the time element, this feast required a special journey to Jerusalem for all the men of the land. It was a time of great rejoicing, for the harvest was now gathered.

The Feast. The Lord said "And you shall count for yourselves from the day after the Sabbath, from the day that you brought the sheaf of the wave offering: seven Sabbaths shall be completed [that is, seven weeks, or 7 x 7 = 49 days]. Count fifty days to the day after the seventh Sabbath [49 + 1 day]; then you shall offer a new grain offering to the Lord" (Lev. 23:15–16).

The new grain offering had a number of distinguishing features:

Firstfruits	*Pentecost*
Barley	Wheat
Sheaf of grain	Two loaves of bread
No leaven	Leavened bread
First of the harvest	Completion of harvest
Wave Offering	Wave Offering

Barley was the food of the poorer people—like

the lad with five barley loaves and two small fish. Wheat, which came up later, was more nutritious and was used by those better off.

While it has been observed that Christ was the Firstfruits of the great harvest, that His humiliation was the prelude to a great exaltation, it must also be seen that the handful of believers who were present at Christ's resurrection were but a small foretaste of the great multitude who will be ingathered at Christ's second advent. In all the work of the Lord, His gifts to His Church and the resultant spiritual blessings are an ever-increasing, truly enriching experience.

The difference between a sheaf of grain and a loaf of bread is that the first is made of separate grains and the second is the same grains consolidated into one loaf. Leaven is in this bread because, although the Lord desires it otherwise, sin is found within the church. It was because of this presence of sin that the sin offering, the burnt offering, and the peace offering were included at this feast.

One of the unexpected turns in the Leviticus passage is that though the subject is firstfruits—new grain that was offered before man could begin harvesting—yet the matter of gleanings is included, and they belonged to the end of harvest. "When you reap the harvest of your land, you shall not wholly reap the corners of your field when you reap, nor shall you gather any gleaning from your harvest. You shall leave them for the poor and for the stranger: I am the Lord your God" (Lev. 23:22).

This law, we should realize, was given to the Jews to influence their personal behavior. It was also given to teach them that the blessings of the Lord did not belong to them exclusively, but some of these were to be shared with other people. Therefore they were to leave behind the gleanings of the harvest. These other people, "the poor and the stranger," could—if we make a spiritual application—refer to the Gentile nations around them.

Today things are in the reverse. The Christian church is enjoying the blessings of the Lord and harvesting the fruits of His saving grace. We should bear in mind that, in so doing, *we* are responsible for leaving the gleanings and the corners for those who are not of this fold. In fact, we should be allowing some handfuls to fall on purpose.

Antitype. The intent of the Feast of Firstfruits is that Jesus is to be recognized as the One who, having risen from the dead, became the Firstfruits of resurrection. When He said to Mary: "Touch me not, I am going to be ascending," He was presenting Himself to the Father as the wave sheaf. After His resurrection He was seen for forty days, proving His resurrection by means of many infallible proofs: "To whom also He presented Himself alive after His suffering by many infallible proofs, being seen by them during forty days" (Acts 1:3).

Just before His departure He promised that when He went away, He would send another Helper, even the Holy Spirit. Whereupon He "commanded them not to depart from Jerusalem, but to wait for the Promise of the Father . . ." (Acts 1:4). One hundred and twenty of those disciples gathered in an upper room to spend the time waiting and in prayer (read

Acts 1:13–15). They were together in that room for ten days (40+10): "Now when the Day of Pentecost had fully come . . ." (Acts 2:1). This was not something new. It was the sixth day of the third month which, according to the Jewish calendar, was the date for the annual observance of the Feast of Pentecost. The day was not new, the feast was not new, but what happened on that day was. And yet not really new; rather, it was the fulfillment of a long-standing type.

What actually happened on *that* Day of Pentecost, when the Holy Spirit came in all the fullness of His power, is seen by comparing the ritual of the Feast of Firstfruits with the Feast of Pentecost. In the first was the presentation of the sheaf, which was comprised of hundreds of separate grains of barley. In the second feast, two loaves of bread were waved. A loaf of bread consisted of grains of wheat ground into flour, mixed with oil, and baked in an oven—and so the separate identities were consolidated into a oneness.

Gathered in the upper room were a hundred and twenty individual believers, men and women who were prepared to be dead to themselves—ready to lose their identity for Christ's sake. They were of one accord when the oil of God's Holy Spirit descended and the tongues of fire rested upon them, and they were fused together into one body—the Church—and thus the New Testament Church was born.

Someone will ask: "Were there not two loaves?" That is true. When the Spirit of God descended on those believers on the Day of Pentecost, He descended upon the Jews only; but later on, in the house of Cornelius, there came another outpouring of His Spirit, this time upon the Gentiles. "While Peter was still speaking these words, the Holy Spirit fell upon all those who heard the word. And those of the circumcision who believed were astonished, as many as came with Peter, because the gift of the Holy Spirit had been poured out on the Gentiles also" (Acts 10:44–45).

Later, when Peter was bearing testimony to the Church Council at Jerusalem, he said: "And as I began to speak, the Holy Spirit fell upon them, as upon us at the beginning" (Acts 11:15). The Lord, foreseeing that there would be two distinct outpourings of His Spirit, ordained that there should be two loaves of bread at that feast; but now in Christ Jesus there is neither Jew nor Gentile—we are one in Him.

Leaven was in those loaves because this Church on earth has never been free from sin. One day it is going to be the Church in heaven. Then He will present it faultless before the Father with exceeding joy.

Spiritual Application—*Enduement of the Holy Spirit.* "For the promise is to you and to your children, and to all who are afar off, as many as the Lord our God will call" (Acts 2:39).

Here is an important subject, concerning which there are many confused minds, and so it demands that we give it honest and careful consideration. Many people will relegate this subject to the past and say that it does not concern the Church of the present day. If we do this, one of the steps that the Lord set out for the Christian walk is being removed. This step is turned into a barrier, so that progress, which would bring us to the end of the journey, is prevented.

Notice carefully that those early Christians were baptized with the Holy Spirit for life and for service. If Pentecost was instituted as a type in the Old Testament and if the Old Testament truth is ratified in the New Testament, then surely Pentecost should be taught today. Not only that, but we should diligently seek it, if we want to see progress and accomplishment in our Christian life and service. To those who would relegate it to the past—to some other age or to some other people—note that the promise was made to the Church at the time of its formation, and we are the people in this Church age. "For the promise [baptism of the Holy Spirit] is to you [there at that Day of Pentecost] and to your children [the next generation], and to all who are afar off [future generations and Gentiles], as many as the Lord our God will call"—so if you have been called to salvation, then the promise belongs to you.

Some may quote Paul that "tongues will cease." To do that is to take a text out of context, for the whole statement reads: "Love never fails. But whether there are prophecies, they will fail; whether there are tongues, they will cease; whether there is knowledge, it will vanish away" (1 Cor. 13:8). Can it be said that prophecy has failed? Dare anyone suggest that knowledge has vanished away? Then on what grounds are tongues removed? In this statement we are by no means supporting a Tongues Movement. Where the genuine exists, the spurious can often be found. There can be no false or counterfeit unless there is a *genuine* somewhere. What we are seeking to do is to be honest with the Word of God.

One other argument should be closely examined: the often repeated statement that the Lord gave "tongues" on the Day of Pentecost in order to enable the disciples to preach to the foreign nationals who were gathered in Jerusalem. This is false. First, the speaking in tongues was exercised by the hundred and twenty disciples initially in the upper room, and there were no foreign nationals in that room. Second, the hundred and twenty did not *preach*. The testimony of all who heard was that the disciples were magnifying the Lord: they were engaged in *worship*. Third, the only person who preached that day, according to the record, was Peter. He was supported by the eleven. Fourth, the only people Peter addressed were the Jews: "Men of Judea and all who dwell in Jerusalem." He did not specifically address the visitors. Therefore, the only tongue he used in preaching must have been the Jewish tongue.

Having said this as a matter of explanation, we will drop it because it is not the subject under consideration. Worshiping in foreign tongues was only an *outward* evidence. Our primary concern should be with what took place *inwardly*.

These people were changed. The timid became fearless, the weak became strong, the coward became brave; lives were changed, they went everywhere preaching the Word, and that Word was effective. The Peter who yesterday could not take the taunt of a servant girl stands and preaches with such power that three thousand souls are saved. What brought about this power? What was the source of this enabling? What was the secret that caused a handful of weak people to turn the world upside down? It was Pentecost. Before this they were believers without power; now they are believers with power.

Beloved, we are believers and we are saints. But where is our power? Let us confess that we have lost out somewhere. The Church needs Pentecost, every preacher needs Pentecost, every child of God needs Pentecost, and the world is dying because there is no Pentecost. The floodgates of God's Holy Spirit have been closed, and we must ask ourselves diligently—on which side of the gates are the bolts? If we know salvation and separation, if we know sanctification, then may we allow the Lord to lead us on to Pentecost. The result will be seen in the next feast.

· Chapter 7 ·

The Feast of Trumpets

Then the Lord spoke to Moses, saying, "Speak to the children of Israel, saying: 'In the seventh month, on the first day of the month, you shall have a sabbath-rest, a memorial of blowing of trumpets, a holy convocation. You shall do no customary work on it; and you shall offer an offering made by fire to the Lord.'"(Lev. 23:23–25)

And the Lord spoke to Moses, saying: "Make two silver trumpets for yourself; you shall make them of hammered work; you shall use them for calling the assembly and for directing the movement of the camps. When they blow both of them, all the assembly shall gather before you at the door of the tabernacle of meeting. But if they blow only one, then the leaders, the heads of the divisions of Israel, shall gather to you. When you sound the advance, the camps that lie on the east side shall then begin their journey. When you sound the advance the second time, then the camps that lie on the south side shall begin their journey; they shall sound the call for them to begin their journeys. And when the congregation is to be gathered together, you shall blow, but not sound the advance. The sons of Aaron, the priests, shall blow the trumpets; and these shall be to you as an ordinance forever throughout your generations When you go to war in your land against the enemy who oppresses you, then you shall sound an alarm with the trumpets, and you will be remembered before the Lord your God, and you will be saved from your enemies. Also in the day of your gladness, in your appointed feasts, and at the beginning of your months, you shall blow the trumpets over your burnt offerings and over the sacrifices of your peace offerings; and they shall be a memorial for you before your God: I am the Lord your God." (Num. 10:1–10)

"And in the seventh month, on the first day of the month, you shall have a holy convocation. You shall do no customary work. For you it is a day of blowing the trumpets. You shall offer a burnt offering as a sweet aroma to the Lord: one young bull, one ram, and seven lambs in their first year, without blemish. Their grain offering shall be fine flour mixed with oil: three-tenths of an ephah for the bull, two-tenths for the ram, and one-tenth for each of the seven lambs; also one kid of the goats as a sin offering, to make atonement for you; besides the burnt offering with its grain offering for the New Moon, the regular burnt offering with its grain offering, and their drink offerings, according to their ordinance, as a sweet aroma, an offering made by fire to the Lord." (Num. 29:1–6)

NO FEAST was observed in the fourth, fifth, or sixth months. These would probably be the hot months of the year.

The seventh month was known as the Sabbatic month. In it the last three feasts were to be observed. These three, Trumpets, Atonement, and Tabernacles, were all included in what was known as "Tabernacles." The last journey to Jerusalem, therefore, involved a stay of three weeks. While the Feast of Tabernacles was on the first day of the seventh month of their ecclesiastical or religious year, it was the beginning of their civil year.

The Feast. This cannot be described like the others, because nothing special happened other than the blowing of trumpets—and that took place at each full moon and therefore was a monthly event.

A brief consideration of the general practice of the blowing of trumpets might be useful. Two trumpets were always in use. These are described in the book of Numbers: "Make two silver trumpets for yourself; you shall make them of hammered work; you shall use them for calling the assembly and for directing the movement of the camps" (Num. 10:2). In later years, and at the present time, rams' horns were used, called *shofars*.

The purpose of these two trumpets was to proclaim or to announce. According to whether one trumpet sounded or two, and according to whether there were long blasts or short notes, the people knew how to interpret the call and how to respond. They would know whether the trumpets were calling them to worship, to walk, or to war. They also knew whether all the tribes were involved or only some of them. They were able to respond to those trumpets as a soldier reacts to the bugle call.

In a similar way God has given to His Church the two trumpets of Old and New Testaments which make up His Word. Through these Testaments He makes known His will and His purposes to all mankind. As the trumpets were made of silver—so the great theme of the Bible is redemption. It is the sweet, clear sound of the gospel. As the trumpets were of one piece—so there is a oneness, an entirety, a harmony, in the whole of God's Word.

The Old Testament comprises thirty-nine books, written over a period of nearly two thousand years. The many writers included kings and prophets, scribes and shepherds, teachers and servants, judges and priests, poets and singers, and others from diverse walks of life—yet the Book is one.

Likewise the New Testament with its twenty-seven books, written over a period of one hundred years, declares truth—recording the fulfillment of earlier prophecies about the future. The writers included a taxgatherer, a doctor, a fisherman, a tentmaker, and others, and yet it is one Book. Like the sound of the trumpets, the sounds and the calls are many—and yet every hearer can understand. To one comes the call to salvation; to another sanctification; to yet another guidance, reproof, encouragement—or whatever are the needs or longings of the individual.

The trumpets were used only by the priests. "The sons of Aaron, the priests, shall blow . . ." (Num. 10:8). Only men with a divine call and the power of the Holy One resting upon them have the right to proclaim the Word of God—men who, according to Numbers 8:6–15, are called, cleansed, consecrated, and commissioned. "And no man takes this honor to himself, but he who is called by God, just as Aaron was" (Heb. 5:4).

This, of course, does not mean the exclusion of men who cannot enter full-time ministry: God can and does qualify men in all walks of life to serve

Him. But it does mean that every individual who seeks to teach the Word of God should not be a novice (1 Tim. 3:6) but one who is aware of God's call and equipping.

Having considered the trumpets and the trumpeters, we should say something about the trumpeting.

The trumpets were always sounded on the Sabbath days, at every new moon, at each festival, and on all special occasions. Some of the purposes for which trumpets were used were . . .

Invitation—for the gathering of the people.

"When they blow both of them, all the assembly shall gather before you at the door of the tabernacle of meeting" (Num. 10:3).

Advance—when the camp should move on.

"When you sound the advance, the camps that lie on the east side shall then begin their journey. When you sound the advance the second time, then the camps that lie on the south side shall begin their journey . . ." (Num. 10:5–6).

Conflict—an alarm for war.

"When you go to war in your land against the enemy who oppresses you, then you shall sound the alarm with the trumpets . . ." (Num. 10:9).

Worship—announcing spiritual events.

"Also in the day of your gladness, in your appointed feasts, and at the beginning of your months, you shall blow the trumpets over your burnt offerings and over the sacrifices of your peace offerings . . ." (Num. 10:10).

Emancipation—a joyful sound at Jubilee.

"Then you shall cause the trumpet of the Jubilee to sound on the tenth day of the seventh month; on the Day of Atonement you shall make the trumpet to sound throughout your land" (Lev. 25:9).

There are other important occasions mentioned in Scripture, so a reminder may help us to appreciate the usage of trumpets. These references are to trumpets other than the two which belonged to Israel. The first sounding of a trumpet recorded in the Bible was at Sinai.

(Exod. 19:13) "When the trumpet sounds long, they shall come near the mountain." The giving of the law was with the sounding of a trumpet.

(Rev. 4:1) "And the first voice which I heard was like a trumpet speaking with me, saying, 'Come up here, and I will show you things which must take place after this.'" Revelation was accompanied by the sound of a trumpet.

(1 Thess. 4:16) "For the Lord Himself will descend from heaven with a shout, with the voice of an archangel, and with the trumpet of God." This trumpet will be the last, because we read in . . .

(1 Cor. 15:52) ". . . in a moment, in the twinkling of an eye, at the last trumpet. For the trumpet will sound, and the dead will be raised incorruptible, and we shall be changed." This will be the final gathering—the call home.

Trumpets have discernible sounds. They are readily understood by those who will listen. They are clarion calls that demand immediate obedience. Paul, when dealing with the Corinthian church concerning the vexing subject of speaking in tongues, said: "Even things without life, whether flute or harp, when they make a sound, unless they make a distinction in the sounds, how will it be known what is piped or played? For if the trumpet makes an uncertain sound, who will prepare himself for battle?" (1 Cor. 14:7–8). This is a call to a clear and distinct ministry, and it is a reminder that the Word of God—the two trumpets—has a clear and distinct message. The trouble is that too many people are too preoccupied to listen, or have an already biased mind.

Antitype. Whereas the previous feasts have revealed historical facts, these remaining three are prophetic. This is accounted for by the fact that there has been a stepping into the seventh or sabbatic month, and also that there has been a gap of three months since the Feast of Pentecost.

These feasts were all Jewish and were, and still are, celebrated by the Jewish people. Therefore the interpretation of each feast is primarily Jewish. However, there is a second lesson or application, inasmuch as they pertain to the Church.

The four feasts—Passover, Unleavened Bread, Firstfruits, and Pentecost (or, Calvary, the Emmaus walk, resurrection, and the outpouring of the Holy Spirit)—are all in the past as history. The three feasts—Trumpets, Day of Atonement, and Tabernacles (or, testimony, second advent, and millenium)—are all in the future and are prophetic. This means that the three-month gap which stands between the historic and the prophetic feasts must represent the present—and that, of course, is the Church.

These relationships are all summed up in two

verses: "He came to His own [the Jews], and His own did not receive Him [Calvary]. But as many as received Him [whosoever will], to them He gave the right to become children of God [the Church], even to those who believe in His name" (John 1:11–12).

Because of this rejection of Christ by His people and the Lord's invitation to the "whosoever will," the Jewish people were dispersed and the Church came into being. The Jews had rejected their Messiah; therefore, He temporarily set them aside. Pentecost ushered in the Church period, so for the Jewish nation there were the three months without any religious feast. They were rejected.

We believe that the Church age is very near to its close. The coming of the Lord is at hand. The sabbatic month is about to begin; perhaps it has already begun.

On the first day of this seventh month there was the sounding of the trumpets, in fact a special sounding of the trumpets so that it became an annual feast day.

Previously the ten tribes had been carried away. At the present time the whole nation, Israel and Judah, is scattered abroad. These people have not been in their land since the days when Titus destroyed the city of Jerusalem and the Temple, and carried them away into captivity. However, today the evidence around us is that this nation has heard the sound of the trumpet, the clarion call taking them back into their own land, for we have witnessed the establishment of the State of Israel—a nation once more.

The prophetic picture that describes this event is in the thirty-seventh chapter of Ezekiel. The prophet was caused to see a valley of dry bones—and the bones were very many and very dry. These represent the Jewish people, who would be buried in the grave-yard of the nations for a very long time.

The prophet was twice asked whether he thought these bones could live, and twice he referred the question back to the Lord. On each occasion the prophet was to prophesy, which he did with the accompanying results. The repeated injunction "Prophesy, son of man . . . so I prophesied" is fitted into this feast, because it could have been "Blow, son of man . . . so I blew." The two blowings would belong to the two silver trumpets.

On the first blowing, bones came together, sinews and flesh came upon them, and skin covered them. The valley then became full of corpses.

I am suggesting that this first trumpet of command has already been heard by God's people scattered across the valley of the world, because bone has been coming to bone as these people have been congregating back in their own land. Sinews, flesh and skin have come upon them as they have developed into a nation—Israel—and are taking a position among the nations; but while they have returned, they are still dead spiritually, for the Lord declared that they would return in unbelief.

At the second blowing, or prophesying, the corpses received breath and stood up—a living army. If the first trumpet has already sounded, the second will not be long after, and its sounding in the prophetic program will be after the Lord has come in the air to take away His Church. This will be followed by tribulation, at the end of which the Lord will come back to this earth, His feet will stand upon the Mount of Olives, and the people will behold Him whom they pierced. It will be both a day of mourning and a day of rejoicing, for they shall say: "Blessed is He who comes in the name of the Lord," as was foretold by the Lord in Matthew 23:39. At this time the nation will be reborn, to become the leading nation of the world: ". . . and I will make them one nation in the land, on the mountains of Israel; and one king shall be king over them all; they shall no longer be two nations, nor shall they ever be divided into two kingdoms again" (Ezek. 37:22).

Spiritual Application—*Testimony*. Trumpets are heralds. They make declarations, but not of themselves. It requires living men with breath in their lungs to take up the trumpets and blow.

Having become living people through the work of the cross, having separated ourselves unto the work of the Lord, and having been filled with the fullness of His Spirit and thereby empowered, we now take up these testaments and—in the power of His Spirit—declare the Word of the Living God with a clear ringing *testimony*.

The world is surely needing someone to give it direction, for it is bewildered and hopelessly lost. Who is this someone? It is you, and I. "How then shall they call on Him in whom they have not believed? And how shall they believe in Him of whom they have not heard? And how shall they hear without a preacher? And how shall they preach, unless they are sent?" (Rom. 10:14–15).

May the Lord give us all a Holy Spirit-empowered ministry.

· Chapter 8 ·

The Day of Atonement

Now the Lord spoke to Moses after the death of the two sons of Aaron, when they offered profane fire before the Lord, and died; and the Lord said to Moses: "Tell Aaron your brother not to come at simply any time into the Holy Place inside the veil, before the mercy seat which is on the ark, lest he die; for I will appear in the cloud above the mercy seat.

"Thus Aaron shall come into the Holy Place: with the blood of a young bull as a sin offering, and of a ram as a burnt offering. He shall put the holy linen tunic and the linen trousers on his body; he shall be girded with a linen sash, and with the linen turban he shall be attired. These are holy garments. Therefore he shall wash his body in water, and put them on. And he shall take from the congregation of the children of Israel two kids of the goats as a sin offering, and one ram as a burnt offering.

"Aaron shall offer the bull as a sin offering, which is for himself, and make atonement for himself and for his house. He shall take the two goats and present them before the Lord at the door of the tabernacle of meeting. Then Aaron shall cast lots for the two goats: one lot for the Lord and the other lot for the scapegoat. And Aaron shall bring the goat on which the Lord's lot fell, and offer it as a sin offering. But the goat on which the lot fell to be the scapegoat shall be presented alive before the Lord, to make atonement upon it, and to let it go as the scapegoat into the wilderness.

"And Aaron shall bring the bull of the sin offering,

which is for himself, and make atonement for himself and for his house, and shall kill the bull as the sin offering which is for himself. Then he shall take a censer full of burning coals of fire from the altar before the Lord, with his hands full of sweet incense beaten fine, and bring it inside the veil. And he shall put the incense on the fire before the Lord, that the cloud of incense may cover the mercy seat that is on the Testimony, lest he die. He shall take some of the blood of the bull and sprinkle it with his finger on the mercy seat on the east side; and before the mercy seat he shall sprinkle some of the blood with his finger seven times." (Lev. 16:1–14)

"Then Aaron shall come into the tabernacle of meeting, shall take off the linen garments which he put on when he went into the Holy Place, and shall leave them there. And he shall wash his body with water in a holy place, put on his garments, come out and offer his burnt offering and the burnt offering of the people, and make atonement for himself and for the people. The fat of the sin offering he shall put on the altar.

"And he who released the goat as the scapegoat shall wash his clothes and bathe his body in water, and afterward he may come into the camp. The bull for the sin offering and the goat for the sin offering, whose blood was brought in to make atonement in the Holy Place, shall be carried outside the camp. And they shall burn in the fire their skins, and their flesh, and their offal. Then he who burns them shall wash his clothes and bathe his body in water, and afterward he may come into the camp." (Lev. 16:23–28)

And the Lord spoke to Moses, saying: "Also the tenth day of this seventh month shall be the Day of Atonement. It shall be a holy convocation for you; you shall afflict your souls, and offer an offering made by fire to the Lord. And you shall do no work on that same day, for it is the Day of Atonement, to make atonement for you before the Lord your God. For any person who is not afflicted of soul on that same day, he shall be cut off from his people. And any person who does any work on that same day, that person I will destroy from among his people. You shall do no manner of work; it shall be a statute forever throughout your generations in all your dwellings. It shall be to you a Sabbath of solemn rest, and you shall afflict your souls; on the ninth day of the month at evening, from evening to evening, you shall celebrate your Sabbath." (Lev. 23:26–32)

THIS was the most important of all the feasts and the most solemn day of the year; a day when, by special sacrifice, a whole year's sins were covered. This, of course, did not take the place of the Passover or make the Passover of less value. In point of fact, it was an aspect of it. It could be said that the Passover was the *manward* aspect and the atonement the *Godward* aspect of the Cross.

The day was unique inasmuch as apart from this day there could be no continual fellowship with the Lord because of an accumulation of unconfessed and unforgiven sin throughout the year; also, because the blood of bulls and goats was inadequate.

This day of humiliation, with its ceremonies, also revealed how holy God was and how distant man was from Him. There was no immediate access to God. God was on one side of the veil and man was on the other side—the outside. The access was limited to one man, once in a year, and that under special precautionary measures. Apart from these restrictions there was immediate death, as with Nadab and Abihu.

That veil, which separated God and man, was a fabric of fine linen thread worked in blue, purple, and scarlet, fragile in itself yet formidable in its purpose. (We do not accept the unscriptural and illogical four-and-a-half-inches-thick theory.) It has been described by C. H. Macintosh: "Neither the Levitical priesthood nor the Levitical sacrifices could yield perfection. Insufficiency was stamped on the latter, infirmity on the former, imperfection on both. An imperfect man could not be a perfect priest, nor could an imperfect sacrifice give a perfect conscience. Aaron was not competent nor entitled to take his seat within the veil, nor could the sacrifices which he offered rend that veil."

This was the Day of At-one-ment. The claims of God that man could not meet, and the needs of man that could not be satisfied, were both settled on this day, creating a oneness.

However, this still remained a temporary provision. It was only for the time being and needed to be performed every year until Christ came Himself to die. It was an atonement, it was a *temporary covering* for sin, it was incapable of *removing* sin. For this reason we must always bear in mind that the *insufficiency* of the Old Testament atonement process brought the Lord into the world. Reference is so often made to Christ's atonement. There is a hymn which says: "Christ has for sin atonement made, what a wonderful Saviour!" This statement is incorrect. If atonement had been sufficient, Christ need not have died. Atonement only covered sin. Redemption removes sin and leaves man justified.

The Feast. There were a number of things God required of both the high priest and the people that day. It was a . . .

Day of Humiliation. On this one day in the year, the tenth day of the seventh month, the high priest laid aside all his garments of glory: the breastpiece and ephod, the intricately woven sash, and the robe with its golden bells and pomegranates; also the holy diadem. "Thus Aaron shall come into the Holy Place. . . . He shall put the holy linen tunic and the linen trousers on his body; he shall be girded with a linen sash, and with the linen turban he shall be attired. These are holy garments. Therefore he shall wash his body in water, and put them on" (Lev. 16:3–4). In this way the high priest was dressed like all the other priests. He had nothing of which he could boast. Outwardly he looked the same as all the priests, although inwardly he still remained the high priest.

Once in the end of the age, the great High Priest, our Lord Jesus Christ, laid aside all the glory that He had with the Father from before the foundation of the earth, put upon Himself the plain robe of humanity and, becoming like one of us, humbled Himself. That is, outwardly and actually Jesus became man, but essentially He remained the divine Son of God because His divinity is something He cannot and will not forfeit. It was a . . .

Day of Imputation. Two goats were taken to become one offering; one was for God and the other for man. There were also a young bullock and a ram. These were an offering for the priest, for he too—like the people—was imperfect and needed an offering. This is how the high priest differed from our great High Priest and how man differs from Him who became man. Jesus needed no offering for Himself and, therefore, He became our Offering.

A casting of lots took place for the two goats. The animal on which the Lord's lot fell became the sacrificial one and had to die. The other became the scapegoat. The sins of the people were confessed as Aaron laid his hands heavily on the head of the goat. This was an act of identification and imputation. The sins of the people had passed to the animal. It was then taken into the wilderness and lost, and as the goat became lost so, likewise, were the sins that it had carried. Jesus paid the price of our sin, which is death—"The wages of sin is death"—and He also removed our sins as far as the east is from the west, to be remembered against us no more. It was a . . .

Day of Substitution. ". . . and Aaron shall lay both his hands on the head of the live goat, confess over it all the iniquities of the children of Israel, and all their transgressions, concerning all their sins, putting them on the head of the goat, and shall send it away into the wilderness by the hand of a suitable man. The goat shall bear on itself all their iniquities to an uninhabited land; and he shall release the goat in the wilderness" (Lev. 16:21–22).

This was substitution, or one taking the place of another. "And the Lord has laid on Him the iniquity of us all" (Isa. 53:6). "For He made Him who knew no sin to be sin for us, that we might become the righteousness of God in Him" (2 Cor. 5:21). It was a . . .

Day of Lonely Service. "There shall be no man in the tabernacle of meeting when he goes in to make atonement in the Holy Place, until he comes out, that he may make atonement for himself, for his household, and for all the congregation of Israel" (Lev. 16:17).

No man was allowed to enter into the tabernacle on that day, save the high priest alone. He went in, a solitary figure taking in the blood of the young bull, first for himself, and then entering again with the blood of the goat which was for the people. How significant that none of the priests, nor other sons of Levi, could be within the tabernacle! Jesus trod the winepress alone, forsaken by God and rejected by men. God had nothing to do with the making of man's first covering (aprons of fig leaves); man had nothing to do with the making of the second covering.

> Jesus, Thy blood and righteousness,
> My beauty are, my glorious dress.

This day was a . . .

Day of Acceptance. On this day alone, with shed blood, the high priest was allowed to pass beyond the veil, while the whole congregation waited anxiously outside. Before passing beyond the veil, the high priest would drop incense upon the censer, and then hold the censer at arm's length inside the veil. When the fragrant smoke from the incense had filled the place and dimmed the sight of the mercy seat and the glory cloud, then the high priest entered with the blood. This blood he sprinkled seven times upon the mercy seat, signifying a perfect acceptance with God through applied blood. Then, taking a step backwards, he sprinkled the blood seven times before the ark, meaning a perfect standing before God through shed blood.

Jesus—having accomplished His work of redemption on the cross—"with His own blood . . . entered the Most Holy Place once for all, having obtained eternal redemption" (Heb. 9:12). "For Christ has not entered the holy places made with hands, which are copies of the true, but into heaven itself, now to appear in the presence of God for us" (Heb. 9:24). It was a . . .

Day of Soul Affliction. "This shall be a statute forever for you: In the seventh month, on the tenth day of the month, you shall afflict your souls, and do no work at all, whether a native of your own country or a stranger who sojourns among you" (Lev. 16:29).

This meant a day of sorrow, repentance, confession of sin, a period of a broken and a contrite spirit. It was a . . .

Day of Rest. "And you shall do no work on that same day" (Lev. 23:28). "It shall be to you a Sabbath of solemn rest" (Lev. 23:32).

We need to stand still and see the salvation of the Lord. We do nothing because we are nothing. It is when we rest from strugglings, strivings, and all the works of the flesh that we can appreciate and appropriate His work on our behalf.

> O give Thine own sweet rest to me,
> That I may speak with soothing power,
> A word in season, as from Thee,
> To weary ones in needful hour.

Finally, it was a . . .

Day of Accomplishment. Such a day surely must have results. "For on that day the priest shall make atonement for you, to cleanse you, that you may be clean from all your sins before the Lord" (Lev. 16:30).

Coming out from the tabernacle to the great concourse of people who waited outside, the high priest lifted his hands in blessing over the assembly and cried: "You are clean from all your sins," and so the day concluded.

Jesus has accomplished the same work and has made the same pronouncement to all who are washed in His precious blood: "You are already clean because of the word which I have spoken to you" (John 15:3).

Antitype. Israel had been at variance with God through many years and many apostasies. There has been no relationship since they rejected Christ as their Messiah, their King. The nation has been scattered, a veil has been over their faces and darkness in their minds. Paul says: "But their minds were hardened. For until this day the same veil remains unlifted in the reading of the Old Testament, because the veil is taken away in Christ. But even to this day, when Moses is read, a veil lies on their heart. Nevertheless when one turns to the Lord, the veil is taken away" (2 Cor. 3:14–16).

The evidence is that, at the moment, there is need of an at-one-ment. This will take place after the Trumpets, when the nation returns to its land and the Lord comes to the Mount of Olives and they recognize Him as their Messiah. Then He will acknowledge them as His people.

Spiritual Application—*The Rapture*. For the believer, this will be the Second Advent of our Lord Jesus Christ. At the moment things are not what they should be; the world is upside down, the Church is lukewarm and many Christians are indifferent. We are undoubtedly in the Laodicean period of Church history, concerning which God has declared that we are neither hot nor cold. The present conditions were outlined by Paul to Timothy: "But know this, that in the last days perilous times will come. For men will be lovers of themselves, lovers of money, boasters, proud, blasphemers, disobedient to parents, unthankful, unholy, unloving, unforgiving, slanderers, without self-control, brutal, despisers of good, traitors, headstrong, haughty, lovers of pleasure rather than lovers of God, having a form of godliness but denying its power. And from such people turn away! . . . But evil men and imposters will grow worse and worse, deceiving and being deceived" (2 Tim.

3:1–5, 13).

There is not a particular here which is not in full bloom right now. Satan is having his harvest. Evil is dominating our social structure and righteousness is suppressed on every hand. The saints in many lands are persecuted for righteousness' sake. Much of the Church is being governed by the world—by the World Council of Churches—when the Church should be governing the world by example and precept.

There is great need for an adjustment, an at-one-ment. This will take place when the Lord returns to this earth. At that time wrongs will be righted, sin will be dealt with, the saints will reign, and the Lord will be honored.

We have been saved—spirit, soul, and body—but at the moment our body is out of harmony. Our body is still carnal, it bears the marks of suffering, it knows the limitations of the mortal; but when Christ comes, the mortal shall put on immortality, the corruptible shall put on incorruption, and our earthly body will be changed into a spiritual body. Our bodies will be in harmony with our souls and our spirits. All the things of the earth, the weaknesses and the failings, will be covered—yea, removed. We shall be clean from everything. Our great Day of Atonement will have come in order to fit us for the Feast of Tabernacles.

· Chapter 9 ·

The Feast of Tabernacles

Then the Lord spoke to Moses, saying, "Speak to the children of Israel, saying: 'The fifteenth day of this seventh month shall be the Feast of Tabernacles for seven days to the Lord. On the first day there shall be a holy convocation. You shall do no customary work on it. For seven days you shall offer an offering made by fire to the Lord. On the eighth day you shall have a holy convocation, and you shall offer an offering made by fire to the Lord. It is a sacred assembly, and you shall do no customary work on it.

'These are the feasts of the Lord which you shall proclaim to be holy convocations, to offer an offering made by fire to the Lord, a burnt offering and a grain offering, a sacrifice and drink offerings, everything on its day—besides the Sabbaths of the Lord, besides your gifts, besides all your vows, and besides all your freewill offerings which you gave to the Lord.

'Also on the fifteenth day of the seventh month, when you have gathered in the fruit of the land, you shall keep the feast of the Lord for seven days; on the first day there shall be a sabbath-rest, and on the eighth day a sabbath-rest. And you shall take for yourselves on the first day the fruit of beautiful trees, branches of palm trees, the boughs of leafy trees, and willows of the brook; and you shall rejoice before the Lord your God for seven days. You shall keep it as a feast to the Lord for seven days in the year. It shall be a statute forever in your generations. You shall celebrate it in the seventh month. You shall dwell in booths for seven days. All who are native Israelites shall dwell in booths, that your generations may know that I made the children of Israel dwell in booths when I brought them out of the land of Egypt: I am the Lord your God.'"

So Moses declared to the children of Israel the feasts of the Lord. (Lev. 23:33–44)

Now on the second day the heads of the fathers' houses of all the people, with the priests and Levites, were gathered to Ezra the scribe, in order to understand the words of the Law. And they found written in the Law, which the Lord had commanded by Moses, that the children of Israel should dwell in booths during the feast of the seventh month, and that they should announce and proclaim in all their cities and in Jerusalem, saying, "Go out to the mountain, and bring olive branches, branches of oil trees, myrtle branches, palm branches, and branches of leafy trees, to make booths, as it is written."

Then the people went out and brought them and made themselves booths, each one on the roof of his house, or in their courtyards or the courts of the house of God, and in the open square of the Water Gate and in the open square of the Gate of Ephraim. So the whole congregation of those who had returned from the captivity made booths and sat under the booths; for since the days of Joshua the son of Nun until that day the children of Israel had not done so. And there was very great gladness.

Also day by day, from the first day until the last day, he read from the Book of the Law of God. And they kept the feast seven days; and on the eighth day there was a sacred assembly, according to the prescribed manner. (Neh. 8:13–18)

THE VERY TITLE of this last feast suggests something of rest and fellowship. While it did remind them of the pilgrimage of the past and God's faithfulness, the joy of the feast was the anticipation of that day when journeyings will have terminated and rest will be permanent.

It was to them as the Lord's Table is to the Christian today. In that sacrament we look back to Calvary and remember what it meant to Christ to bring us out of the bondage of the past and to direct us along this pilgrim way, but it is also "till He comes." We anticipate the time when we will sit with Him and feast on heaven's glories, with none to make us afraid.

It was not only the last feast, which terminated their ecclesiastical year, but it was also the longest feast, lasting eight days, from a Sabbath to a Sabbath. It was the most joyous of all the feasts, coming after the one of greatest solemnity, and thereby made a wonderful consummation. The joyous things of life are always more appreciated when they have been preceded by a dark or difficult experience. "Weeping may endure for a night, but joy comes in the morning."

In Deuteronomy 16:13–14 we read: "You shall observe the Feast of Tabernacles seven days, when you have gathered from your threshing floor and from your winepress; and you shall rejoice in your feast, you and your son and your daughter, your manservant and your maidservant and the Levite, the stranger and the fatherless and the widow, who are within your gates."

This was an all-inclusive feast; no one was left out. It was sometimes called the Feast of Ingathering, because it was the end of summer, work in the fields was finished, and the time had come when they could relax and rejoice.

The evidence is that the nation went a long time without keeping this feast, perhaps 800 to 900 years. This is stated in Nehemiah 8:17: "So the whole congregation of those who had returned from the captivity made booths and sat under the booths; for since the days of Joshua the son of Nun until that day the children of Israel had not done so."

Obviously they could not keep the feast until after they had left their tent life in the wilderness and established themselves in the land, but it is puzzling why they did not put this command into practice until their return from captivity.

The Feast. "And you shall take for yourselves on the first day the fruit of beautiful trees, branches of palm trees, the boughs of leafy trees, and willows of the brook; and you shall rejoice before the Lord your God for seven days. . . . You shall dwell in booths for seven days. All who are native Israelites shall dwell in booths" (Lev. 23:40–42).

For seven days all the residents of Israel left their homes in order to dwell in temporary booths. The purpose of this was to give the people a constant reminder of the forty years when the nation dwelt in tents, wandering in the wilderness with no home. It spoke of how the Lord had made full provision in all things, so that not one good thing had failed. It reminded them that the Lord Himself had become a pilgrim with them and had tabernacled in their midst, leading them by the pillar of cloud and fire, and had brought them into the land He had promised.

Then there was the anticipation. These were a people who would always wander the face of the earth. True, it would be as a result of their own rebellion and idolatry, but in all the wanderings they were to keep this feast to remind them that there would be a day when those wanderings would end—when they would possess their own land, build their own houses, plant their own vineyards, and sit under their own fig trees. The promise was: "There remains therefore a rest for the people of God" (Heb. 4:9).

We have read of the trees to be used in the building of these booths. Nehemiah adds to the number: "Go out to the mountain, and bring olive branches, branches of oil trees, myrtle branches, palm branches, and branches of leafy trees, to make booths, as it is written" (8:15).

Many of the trees used are symbolic. The thick trees speak of shade and of divine protection. The palm has always been the emblem of victory, just as the olive has been of peace. The latter also represents fatness and plenty. The willow of the brook signifies a thriving and a blessed people planted by the rivers of water. All these things, while reminiscent, foreshadow the wonderful millennial age, when men shall dwell in peace and safety and none shall make them afraid.

Numbers 29 lists the number of animals to be used in the sacrifices of that week. The young bulls, diminishing in number from day to day for the eight days, were 13,12,11,10,9,8,7,1. It has been suggested that the decrease to the *one* foretells—in fact, declares—how the many sacrifices of the law would, in the fullness of time, be reduced to the One Sacrifice that would be made once in the end of the age. The anticipated peace would come only through the peace of the Cross.

There is a constant repetition in all of the references to the joy and rejoicing of the occasion, to the gifts sent to each other. On the last day of the feast there were special celebrations and joy. While the sacrifice—the diminished sacrifice—of this day was being prepared, the priest, accompanied by a procession of singing people, went down to the pool of Siloam. There he drew water with a golden pitcher which they brought back to the temple, where the water was poured out into one of two silver bowls at the altar. The other bowl contained the wine of the drink offering. These would be poured out before the Lord as the feast ended.

In this connection, during the Lord's public ministry, He went up to Jerusalem on every occasion when it was required of all the males. One of these occasions is recorded in John and concerns this feast. "Now the Jews' Feast of Tabernacles was at hand. His brothers therefore said to Him, 'Depart from here and go into Judea, that your disciples also may see the works that you are doing. For no one does anything in secret while he himself seeks to be known openly. If you do these things, show yourself to the world.' For even His brothers did not believe in Him.

Then Jesus said to them, 'My time has not yet come. . . . You go up to this feast. I am not yet going up to this feast, for My time has not yet fully come. . . . But when His brothers had gone up, then He also went up to the feast, not openly, but as it were in secret. . . . Now about the middle of the feast Jesus went up into the temple and taught. . . . On the last day, that great day of the feast, Jesus stood and cried out, saying, 'If anyone thirsts, let him come to Me and drink. He who believes in Me, as the Scripture has said, out of his heart will flow rivers of living water.' But this He spoke concerning the Spirit, whom those believing in Him would receive . . ." (John 7:2–39).

Thus the Lord was turning the thoughts of the people away from the shadow to the substance, away from ritual to reality.

Antitype. He who delivered will yet deliver. As surely as God brought them through the wilderness experience, the tent dwelling and the wanderings, and into the Promised Land—a fact they were not to forget, because He had given the Promised Land to Abraham and to his seed for an everlasting inheritance—so surely the Jews are to realize in this present dispensation that they are still pilgrims and strangers. They are still a wandering people often far away from their permanent address.

The apostle writing to the Hebrews said: "Therefore, since a promise remains of entering His rest, let us fear lest any of you seem to have come short of it. . . . Since therefore it remains that some must enter it, and those to whom it was first preached did not enter because of disobedience . . . there remains therefore a rest for the people of God" (4:1–9). That rest is the millennial rest, when for a thousand years they will dwell in peace, and concerning which we read: "Now it shall come to pass in the latter days that the mountain of the Lord's house shall be established on the top of the mountains, and shall be exalted above the hills; and peoples shall flow to it. Many nations shall come and say, 'Come, and let us go up to the mountain of the Lord, to the house of the God of Jacob; He will teach us His ways, and we shall walk in His paths.' For out of Zion the law shall go forth, and the word of the Lord from Jerusalem. He shall judge between many peoples, and rebuke strong nations afar off; they shall beat their swords into plowshares, and their spears into pruning hooks; nation shall not lift up sword against nation, neither shall they learn war any more. But everyone shall sit under his vine and under his fig tree, and no one shall make them afraid; for the mouth of the Lord of hosts has spoken. For all people walk each in the name of his god, but we will walk in the name of the Lord our God forever and ever" (Mic. 4:1–5).

"The wolf also shall dwell with the lamb, the leopard shall lie down with the young goat, the calf and the young lion and the fatling together; and a little child shall lead them. The cow and the bear shall graze; their young ones shall lie down together; and the lion shall eat straw like the ox. The nursing child shall play by the cobra's hole, and the weaned child shall put his hand in the viper's den. They shall not hurt nor destroy in all My holy mountain, for the earth shall be full of the knowledge of the Lord as the waters cover the sea" (Isa. 11:6–9).

Spiritual Application—*Heaven*. The life of the Christian is a journey. This journey we have followed. It is one of achievement and attainment, a going on with the Lord in deeper experiences and fuller, richer fellowship. With Paul we say: "I press toward the goal for the prize of the upward call of God in Christ Jesus" (Phil. 3:14). "Looking unto Jesus, the author and finisher of our faith, who for the joy that was set before Him endured the cross, despising the shame, and has sat down at the right hand of the throne of God" (Heb. 12:2).

May we ask you, reader: Where are you along this wondrous path? Here are the steps: salvation, leading to separation and consecration; then receiving the fullness of the Holy Spirit whereby we bear our testimony, until the Lord comes and heaven is our home.

Having decided what our position is, may we be enabled by the Lord to step forward into a fuller experience.

Oh, walk with God, whilst thou on earth
With pilgrim steps must fare,
Content to leave the world its mirth
And claim no dwelling there.
O stranger, thou must seek a home
Beyond the fearful tide;
And if to Canaan thou wouldst come,
Oh, who but God can guide?

The Feasts of the Lord
· Summary ·

April 14:
   Passover—Calvary—Salvation.
April 15:
   Unleavened Bread—Emmaus Walk—Separation.
April 16:
   Firstfruits—Resurrection—Consecration.
June 6:
   Pentecost—Pentecost—Holy Spirit.
October 1:
   Trumpets—Regathering of Israel—Testimony.
October 10:
   Atonement—Return of Messiah—Rapture.
October 15–22:
   Tabernacles—Millennium—Heaven.

This book was produced by the Christian Literature Crusade. We hope it has been helpful to you in living the Christian life. CLC is a literature mission with ministry in over 50 countries worldwide. If you would like to know more about us, or are interested in opportunities to serve with a faith mission, we invite you to write to:

Christian Literature Crusade
P.O. Box 1449
Fort Washington, PA 19034